Preface

Scene 1, Act 1:

(The group leader stands at the podium and says), "Welcome to Toxic Abuse Anonymous."

(The leader then empathetically continues), "We are not here to cure you, only you can do that. We are here for only two reasons: to let you know that you are not alone in this fight and that you are not crazy. Together, we will find the knowledge and strength to heal and release your trauma bond, restore your trust, build your boundaries, and get you back on the right path to happiness. Please share a little about yourself. Don't worry, we are all here without judgment and understand your pain."

Scene 1, Act 2

(I stand up at the podium) Hello, my name is Adam, and I am addicted to a toxic relationship that has been and is causing me trauma. (Everyone claps, and I sit back down)

CUT! End scene. The Journey begins.

Have you ever chosen to stay in a toxic relationship, hoping your toxic partner will change? More often than not, the actual purpose of the relationship is to facilitate your change. A lifetime of trusting the wrong people, accepting maladapted behavior, lying, cheating, manipulation, and other abuse until it seems it is only normal behavior or even deserved.

Whether it is actually normal is not important. The only thing important is that accepting this behavior is not healthy.

I authored this book after going through a breakup from a toxic relationship. I almost didn't write it. I thought to myself, I am not a doctor or therapist. I am just a life coach, a father, a lover, a failure, a success, a human. Why would people need my story?

But then, I thought about a story that a past acquaintance told to me. The story was about a hero. A pizza delivery person that happened to drive by a burning house and ended up severely injured while saving the lives of three children. This man was not a firefighter or trained to save lives. The fact that he wasn't trained fortunately did not stop him from saving lives. This book is about sharing my perspective and experience, not meant to replace professional care.

Back to the breakup that nearly killed me. This was not like any other breakup; this was a painful withdrawal. In my quest to understand why this breakup was so different from past breakups, I dove into a quest for knowledge. I read medical books, watched videos, and spoke to therapists and doctors. It wasn't until I stumbled onto a popular and quite brilliant content creator named "Khodi Verse" I realized I was addicted to a person exactly like someone can be addicted to a substance. Khodi speaks of alcohol addiction, but as he said the word alcohol, I heard my ex's name in my head. His examples of what an alcoholic goes through in order to become sober were perfectly interchangeable. And so began a fresh path of looking into both my relationship, and my life, which painfully exposed my codependency, and, a special addiction, the trauma bond.

Releasing myself from the trauma bond was no simple task. It became clear that I had accidentally become bonded to someone that was toxic to me. The problem was that just knowing she was toxic to me should have given me the willpower to walk away and be thankful that it was over. It did not. I wanted her back, regardless. It was mentally and physically painful to think it was over. I blamed myself for the downfall of the relationship. I begged and prayed for it to not be over.

It was only when I started studying addiction and trust betrayal that I realized it was time to heal. I learned that regardless of how I blamed others, the only path to healing was to take accountability for my own actions, feelings, and future.

What you are about to read was written in two parts. The first is a collection of perspectives and analogies to help you understand what you are going through and why. The second is a step-by-step process to help you let go of your trauma bond and restore your confidence and happiness. The initial version of the book was not published. It was turned into an online course and group that has helped many people overcome their trauma bond and start living their life free of their toxic relationships.

This book represents exactly what I learned, the thoughts I had along the way, and the steps I needed to take to end my trauma bond finally for good. As an example of my thought pattern and writing style, I offer this first example:

The Time Machine

My grandparents were married for over 60 years. I am sure during those years they had many arguments, challenges, love, sex (that is how I got here), adventures, challenges, and laughs, as well as romance, love, hate, threats, obstacles, renewals, breakups, isolation, along with dull and idle times.

So, when my grandfather died, after 60 years of marriage, no one said to my grandmother, "just get over it, there is plenty of fish in the sea." No one offered advice like just stop thinking about them. They are gone, and you can just move on. Everyone seemed to understand that she had suffered a great, irreplaceable loss and that her life would never be the same. The bitter truth was that she would never hold the once again that she had held for so long. People offered their condolences and seemed to understand the relentless pain of her heartbreak. They didn't carelessly say, "hey, at least now you are free."

Being in a toxic relationship differs from a healthy relationship. The intensity of the relationship is often mistaken for love. After all, if it isn't love, why would it be so intense? So much pleasure, so much pain, it must be love.

However, when my toxic relationship suddenly ended, I should have been relieved, happy, and celebrated even. But I was not. I was distraught, sad, betrayed, helpless, and lost. To make matters worse, no one seemed to understand my loss or my sadness. Friends told me to move on, find another, get over it, and be happy.

They did not realize that this relationship was so intense that somehow, this person I was with magically inserted 60 years of marriage into a five-year span. I could not even explain this to my friends or therapist, that somehow, like in a movie, I had been in some magically horrible time warp with this person I loved, that lasted decades, and then suddenly I reappeared back on earth. My logical friends assured me I was only in this poor relationship for 5 years, and during it, I often isolated going through petty breakups and being ghosted or ignored more than we were together. They were happy about my loss and assumed I would instantly snap out of my pain, and start being me again, happy, making money, being adventurous, and laughing. They were incorrect.

My friends could not comprehend that somehow this relationship, even though the relationship only lasted five years, had every single component of a lifelong relationship in rapid succession. In five years, this relationship had as many arguments, challenges, love, sex, adventures, challenges, laughs, tears, hope, failure, romance, love, hate, threats, obstacles, renewals, breakups, and isolation as a 60-year marriage would have had. I was mourning a timeless event, with no relief in sight.

Most people gave me this advice, just stop giving your energy to it. Simply stop obsessing over the relationship. Just stop thinking about her. In psychology, there is an example known as the "Polar Bear" effect. A patient is told to not think about polar bears for 5 minutes. When I now use this method, I replace polar bear with dogs.

The exercise is simple. We can try it right now.

For the next 5 minutes, stop reading this book and try not to think of dogs in any way. Just sit quietly, and no matter what, do not think of anything having to do with DOGS. Start!

So how did that work out for you? Now we know that the more we try **NOT** to think about something, the more we actually think about it. Apparently, the advice I was receiving was useless. Trauma and heartbreak work exactly the same way. We must prioritize our thoughts and process them to let them go. That is the task at hand, so now I say to YOU...

WELCOME TO

TOXIC ABUSE ANONYMOUS

The Legal Stuff

DISCLAIMER: The purpose of this document is to provide accurate and reliable information about the topic and subject at hand. The book is sold with the understanding that the author is not obligated to provide accounting, legally allowed, or otherwise qualifying services. The author of this book is a certified life coach which is an unregulated profession. If medical, legal, or professional counsel is required, a well-versed regulated specialist should be consulted. The author makes no warranty or any contract whatsoever to the reader.

No portion of this publication may be reproduced, duplicated, or transmitted in any form, whether electronic or printed. It is strictly forbidden to record this publication, and any storing of this material is only permitted with the publisher's prior consent. All intellectual property rights are reserved.

The information shown here and throughout this publication is only opinion and or perspective. Any liability arising from the use or misuse of any policies, processes, or directions included here, whether due to inattention or otherwise, is solely and completely the responsibility of the receiving reader.

Under no circumstances will the publisher be held liable for any compensation, damages, or monetary loss incurred due to the material included herein, whether directly or indirectly. All copyrights not held by the publisher belong to the authors. The material provided here is solely for educational and or entertainment purposes and is therefore universal.

The information is presented without any type of contract or guarantee assurance. All trademarks and brands mentioned in this book are the property of their respective owners and are not linked with this publication.

Copyright © 2022 Adam Swickle

All rights reserved. No part of this book may be reproduced in any form without permission from the author or publisher, except as permitted by U.S. copyright law.

Thank You!

I want to thank so many people for helping me draft this book. My friend Lu Ann has to be first. Your loyalty, friendship, and proofreading made this happen. I also want to thank sincerely the founding members of Toxic Abuse Anonymous, Sara J, Holly, Nina, Jeffrey, Marguerite, Barbara, Brooke, Gabby, Michelle, Jude, Joey Drake, and so many others that stood by my side and lent me strength at my weakest points.

I also want to thank some people that truly gave me inspiration along the way as well, Khodi, Naty, Robyn, Jane, Maria, Michael, David B., Darlene, The Amazon, Sean, Bianca, Linda, Aaron, Lance, Kree, Stella, Grace... along with so many great content providers that help people just for sake of helping.

I will even thank the people that tested my resolve, obstructed me, betrayed, and hurt me. Ashley, Keith, Heather, Andrew, Scott, Ro, and others. I have learned that even if someone gives you a black cloud, there is a gift in it. You have kept me on my toes and forced me to re edit this book until it made sense.

Last, but mostly to my children, without their love, I would not have survived the last 20 years of life nor wanted to without you. Children, you are my life, and I am so thankful for each of you.

Table of Contents

A Story from the Author. 9
The Story of Emily and How I Got My Faith Back 21
Introduction What is this all about? 32
Chapter 1 The Plain Truth 41
Chapter 2 Why Wasn't I Loved? 51
Chapter 3 The Hunt for Love 57
Chapter 4 From Habit to Addiction 62
Chapter 5 Why Did it fail? 72
Chapter 6 The Mask 81
Chapter 7 Pride Cometh Before the Fall! 93
Chapter 8 Boundaries and Self Love 99
Chapter 9 Trust 106
10 Step Intentional Program Introduction 116
The 10 Steps Outline 128
Step 1: Admittance 129
Step 2: Commitment 132
Step 3: Intention 135
Step 4: Affirm 141
Step 5: Expand 143
Step 6: A Simple Test 149
Step 7: Boundaries & Self-Love 155
Step 8: The Big Test 160
Step 9: Share the Knowledge 163
Step 10: GO LIVE YOUR LIFE! 164
Some After Thoughts.... 165
Reference Section: 169

A Story from the Author.

Hello, my name is Adam. I am the author of this book and also the founder of a club named Toxic Abuse Anonymous, LLC. The beginning of my stories will probably baffle you, and you will not see the connection until it is time to see it. Then comes the plot twist and you will see why I wrote it.

I formed Toxic Abuse Anonymous, initially on a social platform named TikTok, as a support group for people that have gone through narcissistic abuse, so that they would not feel so alone, and more importantly, that what they have been through is real, and that they are not crazy. What I didn't expect was that over 250,000 people would show up immediately and start asking me for advice.

I have always been someone that has had a unique perspective on life. Perhaps my personal abandonment issues have played a major part in this, along with a bizarre childhood. I will save that for my next book.

I'd like to share one story, in particular, that is most relevant to this book. This amazing story took me over 50 years to write.

As a young man growing up in the 1970s, before toxic masculinity was a thing, I played with action figures known as GI Joe. The GI Joe figures were military, armed with guns and knives and every accessory for a young boy to imagine being in a war zone, well-equipped for any battle. This is where the story begins because, besides all the guns and knives, the GI Joes often came dressed in camouflage. Dark green camouflage for tropical zones, tan camouflage for desert zones, and white and gray camouflage for snow zones.

Try to stay with me here. I promise there is an "Ah Ha" moment coming, and a complete gasp shortly after. I distinctly remember asking my father, "Why are they dressed like this?" My father always replied, "It is called camouflage." He said, "If they were in the woods or in snow or the desert, you would not see them because they would blend in so well. It would be as if they were invisible." I tried to debate that I could see it no matter where they were. I then took them outside and put them in the grass and I could still see them. My father said, "Well, you know they are there, and this is a controlled environment. In a war zone you could not see them," and I believed him.

Another thing that seemed unrelated, later on in life, every time I went fishing, I could see the fish in the water. However, often when I would say, "Oh my God, look at that fish," no one else could see it. Friends would make fun of me by saying, "I see things that aren't there." Eventually, I chalked it up to either catching a moment that no one else was watching and being very observant, or maybe my imagination was seeing shadows and that there were actually no fish there.

Onward to 12 years old. I was a huge Star Trek fan, and back then in the late 1970s, I had a 19-inch Zenith black-and-white TV. One night while watching with my father, he said he was extremely excited that he was getting a color TV soon. I know that sounds ridiculous now when our phones have 4K screens and billions of colors, but in the 1970s, not so much. So, I asked, "what will be the difference?" He replied, "Star Trek and my other favorite Charlie's Angels were actually in color, but we couldn't see them." I remember laughing and saying, "what are you talking about? The captain's shirt is beige, Spock's shirt is blue, and Scotty's shirt is red." He replied, "Those are good guesses but with a black-and-white TV, you can't see that" and, "you must have seen it somewhere else." I tried to explain to him that I could see it plain as day, even on a black-and-white TV, but he said you must have some superpower because he could not see that at all.

High school came soon enough. No longer were my parents dressing me, or in my case, my grandparents since my parents were not my primary caregivers. Often people would look at me and say what are you wearing? I always replied, "clothes" and walked away. I started feeling like I had no sense of fashion, so I adjusted my wardrobe, and everything seemed to be OK.

I understand none of this is too exciting. As promised, if you're reading this, there is a moment coming that will make you gasp.

So, there I was in my senior year. I had a job selling wallpaper in Oceanside, NY. The job paid a small base salary and a commission for every roll of wallpaper I sold. It only gave you $0.25 per roll unless it was custom wallpaper, then you received $1.00 per roll. The funny part is, even though I was a young man living on his own already trying to finish high school, I was already making thousands of dollars a week selling wallpaper. Nobody could understand how I could sell so much, especially the custom wallpaper. I believed it was because I was such a good salesperson. It may be true that I was a good salesperson, but there was something else going on that I did not understand. Since I worked there, customers often asked for my opinion. I would always say this works perfectly, so they purchased it. Oddly enough, this was always my answer.

And then it happened, a day that would change my life. I was sitting in my health class, minding my own business, when the teacher held up a picture with a bunch of dots on it. Looking at the dots, I could clearly see that there was the number "2" formed out of some dots in the middle of the picture. Being an outspoken person all my life, I didn't bother raising my hand and just yelled out it is a 2! The teacher looked at me and said, "You are colorblind."

I laughed and said, "That's impossible!" He then showed the picture to the rest of the class, and they yelled out 37. For a moment, I sat there and wondered how the teacher got everybody in on this conspiracy joke to make me look like an idiot.

He then walked over to me and handed me the picture and said, "Please read the words at the bottom." It clearly said if a person is colorblind, they will see the number two. If they are of normal vision with no color deficiencies, they will see the number "37", not the 2.

I was, to say, at the least, in shock. I come from a family of artists and photographers, and I sell custom-colored wallpaper for a living. When the teacher realized I was the only colorblind person in the room, he got excited. He then took out a large photograph, which was huge, and laid it across his desk. He then asked several students to come up to his desk and look at the picture. Each student said the same thing, proclaiming, "This is just a picture of a desert taken from an airplane." It was, in fact, a picture of a desert taken from an airplane in the 1940s, during World War II of Africa, during the German invasion of northern Africa.

The teacher then asked me to come up to the desk and look at the picture and tell everyone what I see. That is when I learned the magic. As soon as I looked at the photo, I asked everybody if they were blind? I was looking at tents, planes, infantry, and tons of tanks. I could clearly see everything in that picture. As if the picture were there just for me, but nobody else could see it.

The teacher then explained that all the things I could see were camouflaged, and that camouflage does not work on someone who is colorblind. Soldiers that were colorblind had a special role in World War II, either as bombardiers, snipers, or studied aerial photographs to reveal where the enemy was hiding. For the first time in possibly 12 years, which was 90% of my life at that point, I remembered my GI Joe's, and the conversation with my father. He did not realize I was colorblind and telling the truth! I actually would have seen the GI Joes 1,000,000 miles away because they would have stuck out as if they were wearing neon.

I don't know if you can imagine how many times before that day, I was forced to consider mine and other people's perceptions. How many small debates I had on what I saw, and they didn't, or what they saw, and I could not? Perhaps, therefore, my brain always tries to seek different perceptions, because from my childhood I was seeing things that other people were not, while not seeing things that people were. I believe this exercise and that sort of thinking have spread ubiquitously across all my thought patterns and made me slightly different. One of the most obvious things about me that makes me slightly different is that I notice so many people argue about symptoms, and nobody wants to look at the problem. We will get into that later.

I could tell you a million exciting stories that would happen over the next 35 years, where all of this applies, and you would get a lot of laughs, but that is not our purpose today. I'm going to skip all 35 years and talk about something amazing that happened just recently. Something so amazing that it helped me see clearly.

After incredible success on TikTok with Toxic Abuse Anonymous, I started moving over to Instagram. On Instagram, I have a steady group of people that get together on live-stream, much smaller than the TikTok live events. On TikTok, there are often over 20,000 people who enter my live event. While on Instagram, it's usually lower than 50 people and we can discuss our feelings at length.

One of my coaching clients who had received a lot of help by listening to me, wanted to pay me in kind and help me. That person asked for an address where they could send me something. Of course, I said I didn't want anything, but they insisted. A week or so later, I received a package. In that package was a set of specially designed glasses, Enchroma colorblind correcting lenses, which corrected my color deficiency. I doubted they would work, so I chose to live-stream on Instagram, as it was a smaller setting. I collected the entire group of people, including the person who gave them to me, opened the package, and tried them on.

The effect of putting on these glasses was beyond dramatic. The people at the live event kept saying what do you see? I could not speak at all, and if you knew me, this was a miracle because, frankly, I never shut up. But there I was, speechless.

My hands were trembling, tears were flowing out of my eyes. For the first time in my life, I saw colors, all the colors. The beauty of it stopped me from breathing, and I just stood there looking around, as if I was in a land that I had never been to before. Trivial things that I never saw: flowers that were on trees were not there two minutes ago suddenly were bright pink, rooftops were not brown they were red, grass was no longer dull it was brilliantly green. Everything came to life in a moment of amazement.

I started speaking, and the first words I said were, "this is what all of you live with every day? This is what you get to see all the time. You don't know how lucky you are. The earth is beautiful." I then said, "I always found beauty in everything, but now I know everything is beautiful." And then I asked this question, "with all this beauty, what is it you people are complaining about every day?" Right then, I realized I had traveled the entire world. I had been to Amsterdam to see fields of flowers and walked by them, that I had spent so much time in China, and never had seen the color red. That I had seen majestic mountains and endless oceans, and although they were magnificent, through my filtered eyes, after 50 years, I had missed it all. That my life was a lie, constructed by my perception. I had no way of knowing this because I could only see through my own eyes, and those all around me had no way of knowing because they can only see through theirs. This day changed my life, just from the kindness of somebody that wanted to repay me, for the kindness I showed her.

Something even more amazing was the fact that I do not even know this person's name. The community I formed is anonymous, so people could speak without judgment or shame, and this person wanted to stay anonymous, with no name and no picture. Only a voice to me, and kindness to me. I have made and lost millions, owned large and small companies, traveled the world, raised three children that I enjoyed sole custody of from one marriage, and suffered through another divorce later. I must have had 10,000 friends and associates along the way, and mind you, I am one of those people that it is ridiculously hard to buy a gift for.

Of these relationships, it took a stranger to change my life and give me a wonderful gift. She gave me something more than glasses and color; she had given me the gift of perception. She gave to me the ability to see what I had never seen.

I had always seen the world from my colorblind eyes, and now I could see it from theirs. I had realized the difference and suddenly appreciated that both mine and theirs, without a perspective of which is right, both exist at the same time.

I hesitate to make this longer than needed, but I must say that there were dead leaves all around my yard when I placed the glasses on my face. They were brown and lifeless to me. Death is like that, right? Dull gray, deep brown, or black. It seemed very normal to me until I put on those glasses. Then, magically, all those dead leaves became like well-dressed coffins, and the colors of even death became bright and beautiful. That is the power of perception.

Now, you may have enjoyed this story, but why did I tell it to you? Because my company name, Toxic Abuse Anonymous, is a community of members suffering from narcissistic abuse of one sort or another. They are mostly in what is known as a trauma bond from either a narcissist or someone who is so detached from love that they are completely narcissistic. There is no difference between the two for the abused person. They suffer the same.

On social media platforms such as TikTok, Instagram, and others, there are what we call "lanes." There is a music lane, a joke lane, a dance lane, and so on. A lane is a grouped algorithm that lets users of the platform see more of what they want to see by presenting those categories and carefully tracking what each user is viewing the most of, and then directing more of that content to their screens for viewing. So naturally, this is called the "NARC" lane, and the people that join my page as followers are seeking advice on "narc abuse." The lane has hundreds of content creators, each giving their advice or sharing their own experiences. Some are Doctors, or therapists, some coaches like me, and others that just feel the need to share and be heard. Some of it is helpful, but most of it is just poor advice. But hey, it is free, and in the absence of any advice, even poor advice could be therapeutic.

In this lane, however, there is an elite group that has emerged, the "self-aware narcissist." There are several, with a few reaching "celebrity status" with well over a million followers. I do not have permission to name them, not that they would mind, and they are easy to find if you like.

These narcissists claim to be self-aware, and they are very entertaining, very smart, and quite likable. It is funny to see people ask them, "are you sure you are a narcissist? You seem so nice, and your perspective has helped me to understand my trauma." Those people either forget how nice their toxic ex was in the beginning or just do not fully understand what it means to be a narcissist.

Regardless, let's go back to being color blind. I did not know what anyone else could see before the glasses corrected it. (BTW it is just my nature to wonder if I still really can see color like others, or if the glasses added completely new colors just for me.) So, I knew I was different, but did not know the difference and so lived my life accordingly. I was a "diagnosed" colorblind person, not self-aware. I say that to the community of narcissist content creators, diagnosed, not self-aware. Once I put on the glasses, I became self-aware. I could see as they see, and feel the warmth of the colors, it completely changed the very fabric of my being.

So, I have to wonder if a narcissist cannot truly attach, have empathy, have love. **IF** there was a magical pair of glasses, which could suddenly grant these narcissistic people to see and feel the difference, would they understand the pain that they have caused? Almost any person who has tried to love them ended in pain. Could they withstand the contrast and become what they claim to be SELF-AWARE?

Could they endure being in a room filled with their ex-partners or children and actually feel all the pain they have caused, the loss of self, the denial of validation, the addictive state of desperation they have enabled to exist just so they could get their supply of attention? The actual feeling of heartbreak they would now feel as their own since that is what empathy does. It lets you feel another's emotion as if you were experiencing it yourself.

Assuming they didn't die of heart failure right then, would they then realize (as I did from wearing the colorblind glasses) that they have lived a lie? A life not even worth living, for they have never truly felt love or ever been loved according to their maladapted perceptions. They have lived a life of materialism and shallowness and never had a life of meaning. They, in the same way as I couldn't see color but lived amongst all that could, have lived their life, and have never actually known the difference, just that they are different.

We could then observe and study them. Watch what they thought was their pride turn to shame. What they thought was strength turn to weakness. Listen to their elation, that they have finally found what only others speak of. That suddenly, their life had meaning, that for the first time, they are experiencing joy. The kind of joy only love can supply, the magic of feeling the genuine rush of love. That they finally found out that they too were special, beautiful, and flawed and it was okay.

Life would be more than just a series of activities to give pleasure or pain. How wonderful it is to finally find love, to swear on everything now holy, to change their very essence and do the things that give another joy just for the sake of doing it. How divine it was to feel genuine love, not to just be loved, but to love another. The earth would change to a better place for them in one instant! They are finally blessed! AMEN, Hallelujah!!!

Then and only then, to repay them in kind, for all the pain they caused, snatch the magic glasses off their faces, and return them to the dead vapid vacuum they are, no explanation, no reason other than pettiness, no empathy for them, no compassion, no love, no mercy. They would certainly plead and beg for just one more moment of love, of pain, one more glance, one more chance, one last feeling of hope.

But no, it is not over yet, my readers, no, indeed. As they lay there in endless writhing pain, wondering if they should bother taking one more breath, we shall then blame them for their very existence. We will high-five each other and laugh at them and tell exaggerated stories about them. We will ridicule them to their friends and family, and rejoice as they sit there isolated and alone, in their black hole of hell, just as they did to us.

And as they lose all sense of validation, all sense of worth, as all their own trust and self-respect diminish and disappear, we will simply cast them away, discard them as trash, and let them sit in the trash for all eternity, never to be shown an ounce of mercy. Only then would they know the pain they have truly caused, all to avoid losing their shallow pride, a pride that has cost so many their very soul.

This is the miracle of the gift of those glasses, so thoughtfully given. The contrast between us and them. As people with empathy, with what we call a soul, with grace and even the slightest bit of dignity, we could do none of this to them. Our empathy would make us feel their pain and stop us in our tracks. We would instead, and despite all the pain they have given us, simply smile, and say, "Welcome to the world we always thought you belonged in, and by the way, keep the glasses as a gift." We could do none of the things they thought we could do. The contrast, of course, is that they cannot imagine a world like ours, even though they live amongst us, they are not us. People call them evil, but I cannot. If there is evil, it has surely been done to them. For they are those that can never love, nor ever feel loved.

By now, you must realize two things. First, I am not only the founder of this community, but I am surely also a member. And second, I have felt the trauma bond in full effect, and nearly lost my life from it.

The unbearable pain of loving a narcissist is a pain so bad that we cannot even describe it in words, but we can name it. Some name it abuse, others call it heartbreak, and some claim it as the trauma bond I have named mine, however, as **Emily**.

For it was she that I allowed to insert not only that pain inside me, but also expose the pain that was hidden in there already. I want to add her to the dedication in this book, because the pain she gave me, which nearly killed me, has miraculously transformed into support for literally hundreds of thousands of people, simply by helping them to realize two especially important things:

They are not alone, and they are not crazy.

The Story of Emily and How I Got My Faith Back.

I dedicate this book to every one of my followers that have appreciated me so much, without even knowing that it is they who saved my life. I also dedicate this book to my children, as they give me a reason to live my life. And last, I dedicate this book to Emily. Without her, none of this would have been possible.

Emily: noun

Pronounced: M.L.E.

There I was, alone and single. I was just going through the finalizing of my second divorce. I was turning down dates on Tinder like I was a rock star. Along came this message. "Hey there, how are you? I see you live close. Would you like to go for a drink?"

There she was, a strikingly beautiful woman, asking me to go for a drink, right then... not tomorrow, not next week, right now. I remember asking my son what I should do, he looked at her picture, looked at me baffled, and said, "Damn Dad, Go!" So, I picked a spot, got ready, and left my house, possibly for the first time in months, to meet a woman named Emily.

She was fashionably late that night. I waited in the parking lot for her to pull up. While waiting, possibly the most beautiful woman I had ever seen, started walking towards me from the parking lot. My breath literally left my body as I tried to remain calm and say hello. She walked up, "Hi Adam, I'm Emily" she said. We went inside and grabbed some chairs at the bar. I ordered a Brunello de Montalcino, and it impressed her. They didn't have that by the glass, so I bought the entire bottle.

By the end of the night, I was all in; I knew it. Maybe she did too. She was all out; I thought. I walked her to her car and tried to suggest a kiss by asking how long it had been since she was kissed? She firmly resisted in a very nasty way. I remember confidently asking her, "If she was here, who is running hell?" I got into my car and thought of one thing, "crash and burn." I had blown the chance; my dating skills were zero at that point.

As fortune has it, she scoped out my profile on another platform, and I contacted her. We flirted. She wasn't particularly good at flirting, which was flirting in itself, and arranged a date. Dinner on the beach that week. That very day, she called that her young son had injured himself at camp in Orlando. I offered to drive her. No strings, just drive. It wasn't necessary; she said but was impressed I offered. I remember thinking, if it were my son, nothing would stop me from being there. (I guess being colorblind also stopped me from seeing imaginary red flags as well.) Our date stayed as it was. We had a nice dinner and walked on the beach. She looked at me and said, well if you can't kiss, we need not bother wasting our time. Her aggressive stance surprised me. She then kissed me as if we were in some movie with nothing but moonlight to guide us. I can still remember that kiss, a kiss so good that if right then you told me I will never kiss another, for the rest of my life but her, I would say, "where do I sign?"

The next date was dinner at her house. I was cooking; she does not cook. I made a fabulous stuffed chicken, if I say so myself, and went right back to kissing. Then harmless cuddling, and then she wanted to have sex. I was hesitant, "I do not do casual sex," I then said, "I will pass for now." She, in turn, literally demanded that I do not get to choose things like that. It was her choice. Okay then, it's on. None of this was a warning sign for me. This creature intoxicated me to the point that I could not think straight.

I was being seduced, and I just went with it. Okay, now I knew two things: I never wanted to kiss another woman, nor did I ever want to sleep with another as well. Yup, I was all in.

By the third week of dating, talking, and hanging out, she told me she was in love with me. I can remember my reply. I was shocked and replied, maybe you just think that. Please do not ask me to say that back to you. I knew that if my ears heard me say those words to her, I could never unhear them. I explained to her that if I said it, I would mean it, and I cannot undo that. She didn't mind, so I didn't. But yes, I was already head over heels in love with her. She knew it, she could see it in my eyes.

It took just four more days until I just couldn't hold it in any longer. I confessed I was very much in love with her as well. I was crazy for this woman. Check, she was a mom. She was successful, check; she was brilliant, check; she was sexy, check; she was funny, check; she was gorgeous, check, and every other thing you could check off on a list, she was. I was the luckiest man in the world. Suddenly, every dreadful thing that ever happened to me, every unhealthy relationship, even both divorces, seemed to make perfect sense. If I had gone back in time and changed any event, the stars and the moon and sun would not have aligned to get me right here where I wanted to be, with the woman I had been seeking all my life, my Emily.

Another thing I would like to briefly add to this story. Emmy was the queen of seduction, luxurious trips, great restaurants, exceptional conversations, and, of course, sex. Emmy loved to be romanced, and I love being romantic. She demanded romance and chivalry, regardless of place or time, except in the bedroom. I missed this red flag. In bed, Emmy was a solid 50 if you were using a scale of one to ten. However, romance and intimacy were not allowed. It was like a private freak show you couldn't walk away from. No boundaries were present at any time in the bedroom. Some of it scared me, and while most of it intrigued me, I should immediately have known there was a major flaw in our relationship.

Now at this point in the movie, I could fast forward to the end and tell you how I nearly took my own life, but let's just fast forward 3 days. 3 days after we were again lying in bed, schmoozing away, admiring our newfound love, celebrating, we finally found each other, when I mistakenly said these apparently selfish stupid words. I said, "I haven't felt this way in a long time." She replied, "what?" I repeated myself and said, "I have not felt this way in a long time." She asked, "How long?" I said, "like 20 years?"

AND CUT, that's a wrap, people. Let's clean up the set.

She heard me say, "it has been about 20 years" then she got out of bed, dressed, and left my house screaming obscenities, and calling me names. I begged her to explain, and she screamed at me, "I thought we had something special; this is just what you do with women!" Then slammed my door shut on her way out and poof, she was gone.

I thought I was in a love story, a movie about hope and romance, about love. This is a book about trauma bonds, so everything you just read is just the gratuitous love scene they throw into horror films to satisfy the young men that see the movie.

No, the movie set I was on was a combo movie starring Freddie from a nightmare on Elm Street, Michael Myers from Halloween, and Jason from Friday the 13th.

Now I could keep you here with all the details and red flags I missed over the next 5 years of my life. On how we ended and repaired that relationship over 50 times in just 5 years. But why bother? If you are reading this book, your story is just as good.

You see, Emily was a narcissist (or very narcistic). And even though they all look different, they literally all follow the same handbook. Get someone to give them their trust, their heart, their very soul, and then crush that sucker as hard as they can as punishment for loving them.

Emily would adore me, then hate me, then adore me, then cheat on me, then adore me, then leave me, then adore me, then leave me, then adore me, then ghost me, then adore me, then lie to me, then adore me and then start the cycle again and again. Each time, it was my job to prove I loved her. Each time I reacted to her disrespect, cheating, manipulation, or lies, I had to apologize for reacting that way.

It became my role to apologize for being angry that she hurt me.

It was never on the table to discuss why I reacted that way, nor anything she would do to hurt me, that was not allowed.

For instance, Emmy loves to travel. I merely enjoy it. Every time Emmy felt the need to travel, she would start an argument about something petty, escalate it into a breakup, and then "ghost" me as if I never existed. Her very next immediate move was to go online and book several trips all over the world. Once the bookings were finalized, she would call me and restore the relationship. Then laughingly apologize that she really thought the relationship was over and acted accordingly. She would confess she sought other men for comfort, and that she now had a full schedule of traveling.

She would then use the restored relationship to secure me as a babysitter for her children and chauffeur for her trips. Naturally, not wanting to start another breakup and to prove my undying love for her, I agreed. The worst part was that during her extended trips, she would break up with me again, so that she could be unfaithful, only to restore the relationship right before she returned. I am sure she is doing this to whoever my replacement is, as well.

Like you, each time I went back to her, and to maintain the relationship, I fell deeper in love with her. It was the only way to keep her, the only way to satisfy her. I had disclosed to her I was abandoned as a child, and that it was so painful that my mind cannot accept the thought of abandonment, so it converts and hides the act of abandonment into the words "I miss you."

To not feel abandoned, my mind tricks me into thinking I am not abandoned. I just miss them. This was a fatal mistake to tell her. She promised that even in the worst of times she would never abandon me, her love of loves that she adored so much. Her immediate mission then became to ghost me whenever possible for whatever possible. It was torture. Triggering a painful abandonment issue is extremely dangerous and makes people want to end their life altogether just to avoid the physical pain of the event.

She abandoned me so many times that any reasonable person would think it would become a dull pain, but no, she invented new ways to do it. To drop me from higher elevations, to ensure I would suffer, and then beg her to stop.

For example, she gained the knowledge that my deceased mother would always call me "my Adam." Now, even though it was my mother that had abandoned me, a child does not stop loving the abuser, the child stops loving themselves. Blames themselves for the event. I was no different.

So, when Emily learned of this knowledge, she started calling me, "MY ADAM."

By calling me that, it would hurt twice as hard when she would toss me away like garbage. I almost want to blame myself and have many times, but then I thought of each one of her past lovers, at least the ones she and others have told me about. All the people that ever said, "I love you," to her have suffered, and I have nothing in common with any of them except our undying love for her. When I think of all these people, and there are plenty, all suffered as I have. She called them all crazy; she was a victim of these monsters. No matter what, I would never leave her. I would never want to hurt my Emily like all the ones in the past had. I was stupid, I was blind. I was foolish, and I was abused for it.

I now believe what she was doing had to be intentional, to make a person like me get angry at God, just by letting me wake up the next day. To make me feel pain, that God did not show me mercy and take me while I slept.

No need to go into all the pain this person has caused, how some people are literally not on this planet anymore because of her actions, and that they have sent some others halfway around the planet to China escaping her lies. Everyone has a story; this one is mine. Trust me, I am no saint in the story either; I have my set of flaws. Was Emily an actual narcissist? I do not know. Maybe her abusive childhood gave her a "dismissive avoidant" attachment style. If you took an actual narcissist, and a dismissive avoidant, and put them in a room of doctors, it would take them years to decide which is which. Both are so narcissistic that it is impossible to tell one from the other without actual brain scans.

The common denominator here is narcissistic behavior. The complete lack of empathy and the complete discount of love. No, to Emmy, "love" is not a currency. It is of zero value to her, and this applies to me, her past lovers and ex-husband, and her children that constantly ask her why she hates them, while they beg for "useless hugs" as she would claim. Her employees, her staff, her friends, and her family say she is great and then talk about her behind her back. She also spreads rumors about them and truly hates them all behind their backs and uses them so casually while bribing them with expensive alcohol, fancy trips, food, and, of course, money. Not even her dog, which waits endless hours for her to be let out, can serve as an example of her loving something. Nobody escapes her lack of love. Like all narcissists, they are so good at lying and putting everyone in their designated compartment that no one gets to see it from above. The circus ringmaster and her monkeys.

So, what is left to say about this horror show that you do not already know from your own experience with your narcissistic person? Just this, my pain from her final discard, was endless. I admittingly convinced myself that I could not breathe without her. I absolutely loved no one on the planet like I loved this woman.

So, to understand her better, I dove into knowledge. I dove into everything I had learned in school about psychology; I dove into friends that are trained doctors, and I dove into medical journals to read studies and white papers, things that even most doctors would never review. All to grasp the horrible truth, that some people exist, that do not have the capability to love another. That they do not have the actual

DNA trait to trigger bonding or any type of attachment to anything. It felt as though I was a six-year-old finding out that there was no Santa Claus. I felt like the world had let me down, that my faith was crushed. No, she never loved me at all. She is incapable of love.

But knowledge gave me the power to understand there was no one to blame. You cannot blame a wolf that hunts a lamb. And the wolf doesn't consider a cute, cuddly lamb less appetizing and lets it go. No, it just rips it to shreds and eats it. That is its true nature and serves a purpose, as does Emily. Her lack of feeling of true love exposed my deeply buried problem.

I was completely codependent. My self-value was completely based on whether or not someone loved me. I would rather put up with abuse than lose this person.

Once my codependency was truly exposed, I had to learn to forgive myself, learn to have proper boundaries, and stop this crazy cycle entirely. She made me face my abandonment issues as a full-blown effect and finally deal with them as an adult, not a scared child. Ultimately, she cured me of them altogether. Regardless of the pain, I was still here, and the earth was still spinning. A new perspective, a new me.

So, in the end, she lost the one that genuinely loved and understood her. I lost someone that never loved or bothered to understand me. I lost nothing. For we are love, and nothing without it. Creatures such as her have one destiny. I have seen it with my own eyes. As the beauty and youth fade and the patience diminishes, fewer and fewer people tolerate their lies and phoniness. Until literally everyone they know quietly gives up on them, and they become increasingly bitter, and one day die miserable and alone.

I am thankful for her and still treasure our good times. At one point, I lost all my faith in humanity and God. I believe she did this to me on purpose as she hated my God, the Jewish God that forgives everything. I could not understand her racial stance, as her "god" started as a Jew, did he not? She truly does not believe in any deity, which is what enables her to be so cruel to her victims, any faith at all would compel her to lower her useless pride and just apologize, if not at least try to make amends for all the pain she has caused people. If her surrounding people truly knew anything about her as I do, they would run away fast and never look back.

And as I lost my faith in my God, I turned to other gods in my despair. I am not a religious person; I am simply spiritual. They say religion will teach you to stay out of hell. Spiritual people were already in hell and just never want to go back. They leave hell carrying water buckets to help those still sitting in flames.

I tried to pray to my God. I asked God, "God, why do you let people suffer?" No answer, no answer at all. Maybe I had to pray to some other God? So, as I prayed to Muhammad, Hindu Gods and Zeus, and even RAA, I asked them to help me understand how they could allow so many to suffer. I received no answer and no comfort. Finally, I circled back to Yahushua, or Jesus, as the world renamed him, and said these words, "Yahushua, you were a tribe member, one of us, and they punished you for begging them to just forgive and love each other. I am being punished for begging one of your followers to forgive and love me, as are so many others. I know you died for this cause, so why do you let it continue? Why do you let all these people suffer?"

Right then, an answer came to me. No, I didn't hear a voice, no magical appearances, just a simple answer, as this very thought crossed my mind... What would Jesus say if he had actually appeared? His answer would certainly be,

"Adam, I have given you so much experience, which has turned into so much wisdom. I have given you the gift of being able to express yourself and share this wisdom. I have provided you with all the tools to gain the needed knowledge and the painful truth. Yet I have left you with enough grace to truly forgive and not blame anyone or even be bitter. I have given you the willpower and the courage to share the story, and not be ashamed of even the worst of it."

"So, I ask you, Adam, why are you letting them suffer? They need your help and everyone else like you to help them understand they are loved by all but themselves, and that needs to change. So, change it."

That day, I made a single video on the TikTok social media platform, to start a small group, for people to express themselves, a community if you will. What I did not expect is that a quarter of a million people would join the community almost overnight and say these words to me. "Please help me."

And so, I am trying my hardest to help them, simply because I can in some way, help them see they are not alone, they are loved, and that it is going to be Okay.

That is my story, and that is how I got here, by losing nothingness and gaining everything, including some exceptionally good friends from the ashes and my faith restored.

Thank you.

Introduction
What is this all about?

Welcome to a perspective and program to help you learn how to heal from your past, or ongoing relationship trauma. A person who has been through experiences similar to yours wrote the following pages and found a way to heal and grow stronger.

ABUSE is never the victim's fault. Please do not place blame on yourself or the person being abused under any circumstances. If you have been sexually abused or physically abused, please seek a licensed professional to guide and counsel you through the abusive events and help you heal your trauma. This book is about overcoming abuse and betrayal of trust, not physical or sexual abuse.

Also: This program mentions the word narcissist often. A true diagnosed narcissistic personality disorder person (NPD) is exceedingly rare, and there are so many attachment styles and disorders that mimic an actual narcissist that it would take a team of trained doctors' years to actually diagnose the difference because the traits and behaviors of a narcissist are so embedded in so many disorders. Let's not try to diagnose the toxic person you were with by trying to put a label on them. All we really must do is realize you are the victim of a "narcissistic abuse" pattern, and it has caused you trauma that needs to be addressed.

It's no accident that the name of the author's community is Toxic Abuse Anonymous. I named it after an incredibly famous & successful program, known as Alcoholics Anonymous, and just like Alcoholics Anonymous, none of the members ever thought they would be there; none of the members ever wanted to be there. Once the members entered the program, NONE of them thought it would work for them, nor that it could heal them of their addiction or habit.

For many alcoholics, a couple of harmless drinks, which made them feel better, turned into the worst thing they could experience. Their suffering, derived from the need, desire, and *alcohol addiction*, practically destroyed their lives. It was at that very point, that they joined a community group designed specifically to release them from the addiction to alcohol, the actual habit of drinking that took over their lives and showed them a better purpose, a release from the bond that they had with something so toxic.

Perhaps you've met someone that made you feel better? Perhaps you've met someone that seemed so perfect, your best friend, twin flame, or soulmate and you would do anything for them? This person made you feel so good, cared for, seen, understood, and so loved that you just wanted more of them. At that point in the relationship, you couldn't get enough of them. They gave you nonstop attention. They paid attention to everything that you have said and done, down to the smallest details. You were fond of all the same things.

What you did not know is that you had become bonded to this person through trauma. A seduction known as love bombing.

This kind of unconscious bonding caused you to become attached to this person and was done in part, intentionally, by the toxic person only to help themselves. (Much like any addictive substance or activity, the substance or thing is inanimate and does not share your bond.)

An Old Short Story

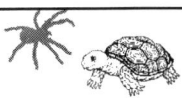

There was once this turtle minding its own business, sunning itself by the river side. Along came a tarantula, noticed the turtle, and approached it. The spider then began to ask the turtle for help in crossing the river. The spider claimed his friends and family were on the other side of the river and he simply needed a ride. The turtle, alarmed by the spider declined. The turtle said, "You are a tarantula, you will bite me! I do not trust you."

The spider replied, "There is no need for your distrust, I am only a harmless spider, I do not nor cannot eat turtles. We simply feed on small insects. Please trust me, I need your help!

Finally, the turtle gave in and instructed the spider to climb onto its shell. Off they went to cross the river. As they crossed the halfway mark however, the spider bit the turtle's neck. The turtle turned to the spider and said, "Why would you do that? Now we will BOTH die!"

The spider simply replied, "I couldn't help it. It is my nature."

Now with the story in mind, let's look at your toxic relationship. Over time, those once wonderful moments of elation have changed into moments of unease, fear, and anxiety. Perhaps those feelings of being loved and understood became weaponized and used for ill intent and manipulation.

What once felt so good and abundant through the relationship honeymoon stage was then suddenly sporadic and in small doses, if any at all. How could something so unbelievably amazing and too good to be true turn into a horrible habit of lowering your standards, boundaries, and self-respect?

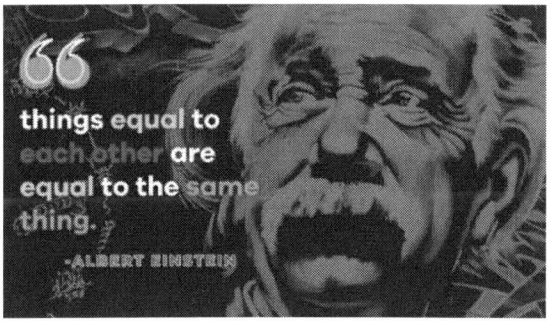

Simple. It was the only way to keep the relationship existing. Suddenly, you are walking on eggshells whenever you are around this person, trying not to trigger them or cause anything that could equate to an argument. You still love them, but now you also fear them. You live in a minefield.

You find yourself wishing that they go back to being who they were in the beginning. I am here to explain this one horrible truth. This is who they truly were in the beginning.

Very much like an alcoholic knows that alcohol is not good for them, and yet they still crave it. Wanting to be in a toxic relationship is an equal nemesis that needs a careful plan to overcome it.

You might ask yourself at this point, won't time cure this? Isn't this just a broken heart like all the other times? The answer is complex and offers no comfort. Yes, you might have a broken heart, which will cause sadness for sure. However, sadness alone will not cause you to feel invalidated. You feel betrayed because you feel so frustrated and confused. The painful frustration portion of your pain is more than likely stemming from the betrayal of trust and self-respect.

Yes, this relationship might have betrayed your trust, which will add to your frustration in the form of anger, but the trust we will discuss is quite different. The trust issue we must face is sourced from within and has created an internally driven doubt. A doubt forces you to feel that you cannot trust your own decisions any longer. You have possibly lost your ability to be convinced of anything, nor have confidence in your ability to complete tasks, including the simple ones that somehow used to be easy. You might feel anxious, confused, hurt, and even depressed.

The hardest emotions you are confronted with are a sense of loss, losing your sense of self, not caring about yourself, trying to understand what has happened, and where did I go wrong? You now have the daunting task of putting the pieces back together, your pieces, while trying to maintain your career and family life.

You might now feel as if they locked you in a private invisible prison, trapped within the walls of your mind. It's not a hardened prison that we see on television or in movies, but in one's mind, it is a safer alternative, where isolation helps numb the pain and has become a haven for you to hide from the world. In this haven, you have pleasures that comfort you, like delicious foods, cable tv, and a soft couch, a "velvet prison."

Let me remind you of something. If you misbehave in an actual prison, they punish you with isolation. But not here. You have created this solitude of safety to protect yourself from the world you once had known and loved. You seek a place of comfort during this time of uncertainty, hurt, betrayal, suffering, and confusion.

How did this happen? You ask yourself. How did I go from going on a wonderful date looking for love to searching the internet, looking for what is going on? How did I go from feeling in love to feeling lost, and becoming addicted to the chaos that has now become the norm in my life?

That answer is complicated. At some point. You must have said these words to yourself, "I'm going to do whatever it takes to make this relationship succeed, period." As soon as you said this to yourself, your brain started to rewire itself and overwrote every single healthy habit that you've ever learned.

The first one that you might have written over or even replaced, was that you actually "need" this other person, instead of just needing yourself to be complete. Is this why you are isolating yourself, to correct this error? Is it that now you believe you do not need anyone? The very next one that you incorrectly replaced was that this was the only person you needed. Why? Because they pretended to fill a void in your life, whether or not you had one.

I'm sure that if you look back over your life from a very honest point of view, you will see the beginning of these beliefs manifesting from your childhood. Parents are not perfect. They make mistakes also, and they make many along the way. We find that most parents did not get married or stay together because they were in love. They got married because they became familiar with the uncertainty of their relationship. They stayed together out of habit. Often people stay in relationships, not for love but because of the comfort and repetition of a habit and nothing more. Ask yourself, are you really in love with this person? Is it the person you are craving, or do you miss your habit?

I wrote this program to help you overwrite an extraordinarily strong addictive habit, mainly the habit of thinking about your ex-spouse, friend family member, with a new habit that will improve your quality of life and create a natural rejection of the old habit. We could use it to replace any bad or toxic habit. However, this one has been written to help specifically with breaking your trauma bond, which is so strong it is equal to addiction.

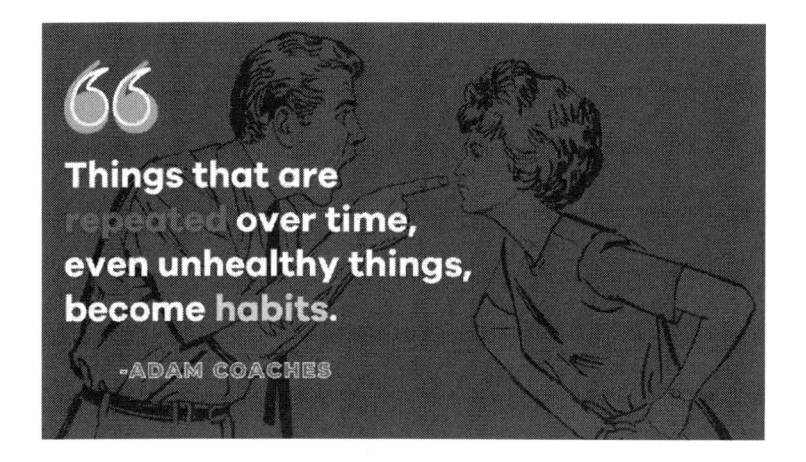

> **Things that are repeated over time, even unhealthy things, become habits.**
> -ADAM COACHES

One more thing, the following lessons include a perspective that can get very technical. This was my way of learning and coping, so I am sharing it with you. If you have no interest in the why part and only the desire to learn how; skip it. That's right, I shared it so you would gain strength from the knowledge and gain a new perspective on what you have been going through.

None of this is a medical dictionary or meant to conflict with what you believe in. I simply provided it to add a new perspective so you can understand it through my eyes.

The program itself, which follows, will still work if you are determined to finally let go of your trauma bond. Are you ready?

Let's begin...

Chapter 1
The Plain Truth

Picture yourself as a bank. Instead of money, however, you have an enormous vault filled with love, light, empathy, and kindness. Banks have long-term loyal customers, generational customers, short-term customers, and walk-in customers. They sometimes get great reviews, while other times they get horrible reviews. They also occasionally get robbed.

Most customers of the bank are depositing money, storing valuables, or withdrawing money. The customers perform these transactions according to the bank's rules and procedures. They do this because they trust the bank to hold their valued property. The bank also has procedures to make sure the people they do business with are trustworthy. People that are not willing to follow the bank's procedures are prevented from being customers. These are the bank's boundaries.

It is clearly the bank's responsibility to make sure the valuables and trust that is held by them are safe. If a bank is robbed, it is not the banks' fault, nor are they to blame. However, it is their responsibility to safeguard its holding, and ensure they do not get robbed again, and also it is their responsibility to replace what was stolen. To safeguard that the bank does not get robbed, the bank usually enlists guards, locks, alarms, passwords, etc. The worst part of a bank robbery is that it happens regardless of security protocols, bank. An inside job.

A quick, funny story about the inside job you may relate to. Two lawyers that are partners are out to lunch. One gasps, "Oh my God, I forgot to lock the safe!" The other looks at his trusted partner and says, "What are you worried about? We are both here."

Let's go back to you. You are like the bank. You hold something extremely valuable, love and trust. We assume our love and trust are safely secure; however, once in a while, we get robbed. Just like the bank, it is often an inside job, or a missed security protocol (a missed red flag) and is not our fault. Even if the thief is caught, however, does not always return the stolen goods, nor protect us from being robbed again. Finding the blame is only useful if you understand how it happened, not who did it, so you can prevent it from occurring again. Just punishing the criminal will not secure your bank against future robberies. Understanding how the criminal could bypass security measures is not the criminal's responsibly, it is yours. So, let's figure out what happened and how to stop it from happening again.

If you wanted a degree in psychology that specializes in toxic behavior, you would have gotten one by now. Unfortunately, as part of the healing process from any toxic habit, unhealthy habits, addiction, or "Bond," you must attain a certain level of wisdom, a knowledge base of what is going on inside your head. If what's going on seems so complicated, it is because you do not understand it.

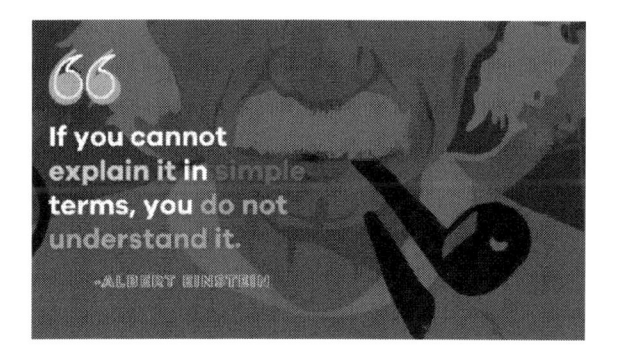

> **If you cannot explain it in simple terms, you do not understand it.**
> —ALBERT EINSTEIN

The lack of understanding causes frustration. Frustration is wonderful, simply because the pain of frustration causes growth. All personal growth stems from frustration.

But what if the truth is very painful? There is power in knowledge, and yes, the truth may be painful, **but the truth will also set you free.** So, for the beginning of this program to have a positive effect, **you will have to learn about some harmful truths, truths about whom you loved, and some truths about yourself**. If you're not ready for this; then stop reading now, because these words will not help you until you are ready to understand some painful truths.

If there is something in these lessons that comforts you, I am happy for you. If something in these lessons makes you *uncomfortable*, then I am thrilled for you! That is the very thing you will need to concentrate on. That is the issue you have been avoiding for far too long, and it is time to address it.

I'm glad you're still reading. **The first thing we are going to understand is the person who you were or are in love with.** I wrote this program to address a relationship with a narcissist or a narcissistic person, as they are the same when it comes to abuse. The program will carry the most meaning if they are a true narcissist. If they are just toxic and narcissistic, the program will help just the same. If they were not toxic at all, but the relationship itself was toxic, this program should be amazingly effective. It doesn't matter what label you want to put on the person you were with, all that matters is that you stop wanting to spend your life thinking about a toxic relationship that could have never worked. To help you understand what you might have been involved with, the next section contains simple-to-read understandings of the overly complex problems that burden some people, and how it effects mating, friendships, and significant others.

Please use the reference at the end of the book to understand and recognize the behaviors of each, and perhaps notice some of your own toxicity in the process. They all share a sense of immature coping styles that can lead to aggression, restlessness, anger, insecurity & irritability which leads to lashing out at their intimate partners, friends, coworkers, and family:

Cluster B Personality Disorders: Cluster B personality disorders have a combined estimated prevalence rate of 1.5 percent of the general population, according to The Diagnostic and Statistical Manual of Mental Disorders **(DSM)** estimates. (120 million people)

All personality disorders are deeply ingrained within the mind. The disorder creates a rigid way of thinking and interacting with people, which has a profound impact on an individual's relationships and mental health. It also affects the well-being and mental health of those with whom they are in close & intimate relationships with. Individuals with cluster B personality disorders often have difficulties maintaining healthy relationships and may display emotional and impulsive symptoms daily.

Of course, there are so many more personality issues. However, these seem to cause the most amount of trauma bonds in the current population. The challenge has always been that each issue has cross traits (co-morbidity), and it is often too challenging to differentiate between a true narcissist and simply Narcissistic Behavior. Sometimes the behavior is so deeply embedded into a person who it cannot change unless that person genuinely wants to change.
The effect, however, is that whether they are an actual narcissist, does not matter! You have still suffered from the behavior.

Your abuse has a name, it is called "**narcissistic abuse**" regardless of what the abuser's diagnosis is, and almost always creates a "**Trauma Bonded**" victim. This is where we will focus all our efforts and energy on healing your trauma, not diagnosing them.

The inherent recurring problem from these relationships is no coincidence. Each of these disorders creates what is called cognitive dissonance, a paradox, if you will. Where two opposing logical thoughts exist at the same time. Just being human makes us mathematical. Things must add up.

If I say 5 + 5 = 10, you will agree because it adds up, but if I tell you 5 + 5 = 11, you will not agree, because it does not add up. In a trauma bond, you find yourself saying, "they love me; I love them, shouldn't that be enough for a good relationship?" Unfortunately, what we never consider is that one party involved does not have the same definition of love that we do, which is universally accepted by most people. **We naturally assume that love means somebody will put another's priorities, desires, and needs in front of their own, based solely on the purpose of love.**

Unfortunately, this is not always the case. This is one of the painful truths you will have to face. That all people do not share the accepted romantic historical purpose and meaning of love. The fact is, most healthy people have empathy, the ability to bond and feel another's emotions. To feel someone else's emotions as if they were experiencing them ourselves. Some people will call that just intuition, others will claim it is

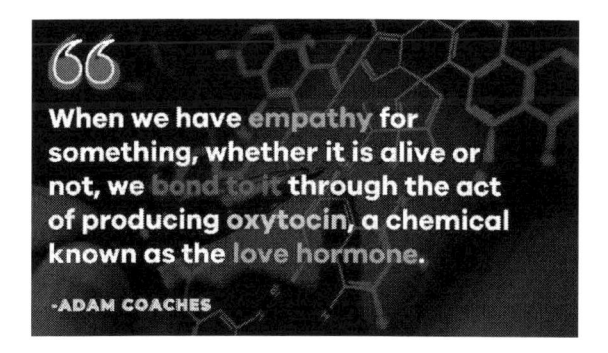

> **When we have empathy for something, whether it is alive or not, we bond to it through the act of producing oxytocin, a chemical known as the love hormone.**
> -ADAM COACHES

magical. The truth is, it has been present in human beings for hundreds of thousands of years and is vital to our survival.

When we have EMPATHY for someone or something, whether or not it is alive, we bond to it by producing the hormone OXYTOCIN, otherwise known as the "cuddle" or "Love" hormone.

This special hormone is most obvious with a mother bonding with a new baby. This bond is necessary to protect the baby, and to prioritize the baby's safety. Without that bonding, the infant would need to survive on its own, so our instinct through bonding protects and gives us a long-term commitment to the baby. But what about the father? The father also produces oxytocin, which the male figure uses to bond to mother and baby, driving the male figure to provide and protect both as a family unit. Times have changed and there is no longer necessarily a need to be male or female roles in this process. Early humans needed this for millenniums of procreation, which has now evolved to no longer needing both roles for anything but the pregnancy itself.

Even though the bonding hormone was initially necessary for humans to survive, it now serves a different role in the advanced civilized culture. It provides long-term bonding even if there is no intended pregnancy, and for the survival of what we now call a healthy long-term relationship. Why would anyone want to stay in any long-term relationship?

There are so many choices, and long-term relationships offer so many obstacles and challenges. You could spend your life seeking new mates, and whenever a problem arises, just toss it away and find another mate. There are now eight billion potential mates on the planet. The answer is bonding. Humans receive pleasure from the release of dopamine.

Finding a new mate releases the dopamine in massive quantities. Healthy humans can convert that release from finding a new mate to staying with a new mate. This is our "healthy" definition of genuine love.

Once you are bonded to a mate, your desire to move on, to find another, is substantially reduced and it converts into higher rewards for overcoming obstacles as a team. With each obstacle defeated, the bond gets even stronger. If you survive enough obstacles together, the bond becomes unbreakable. A "**habit**" of being together has formed, and it is so strong that no other habit or behavior is even thinkable.

However, as in any situation, there is an exception to the rules. What if the person you were with did not actually bond? What if they did not even know what bonding felt like? What if their entire life, love, was nothing more than a short-term feeling of pleasure, to be disposed of as soon as it did not feel pleasurable or became inconvenient?

What if their definition of love differed completely from yours?

That is exactly what a narcissist or narcissistic personality person is, a person who cannot form any long-term bond with anyone. To them, love means weakness, vulnerability where it should mean strength. It means they can use you however they please. So, every time you said the words I love you, they heard, "go ahead and abuse me" and maybe even, "now I can abuse you."

Since this is a program to end your trauma bond, I will end this lesson right here to not keep going on with "*what is a narcissist*" because this is not about them, it is about you.

Chapter 2
Why Wasn't I Loved?

Let's look at the idea that a 4-leaf clover is lucky to find. We all know how rare four-leaf clovers are. It is lucky to find just one. There are millions of acres of fields filled with clovers, all of which have three leaves (the common clover) but then you come across the four-leaf clover.

How exceptional, how rare, how unbelievable that amongst the billions of clovers, you've found the four-leaf clover. Have you ever considered what created it? It is a mutation. It differs from the rest, and the reason it is different is that it is a mutation that happens, yet the mutation itself cannot multiply or have offspring. It lacks the reproductive DNA to reproduce. So, it stands alone in a field of billions, with no possibility of mating, it lives and dies alone.

Let's look at your relationship. You have bonded with someone and seek togetherness. You seek love and compassion, and passion. The mate you have chosen, however, even though they look like all the rest of us, was unique. So different that you considered at one point, that you were lucky to find them in the first place. What you did not, and could not possibly know, is that the very long-term bonding components that have made humans survive were not present in this person. To you, they were the four-leaf clover, and how lucky you are to spot one amongst all the others.

If you found a four-leaf clover, you would treasure it, and eventually store it away to show future generations, without ever considering that a four-leaf clover is rare because it lacks things the other clovers have, the extra leaf means nothing. The person you bonded to was unique as well. They are perfectionists at making you feel lucky to know them. They drive euphoric feelings immediately, as if you found the one-in-a-million person for you. What you did not consider while being seduced is the reason they are so good at this skill is because they have performed it so many times before.

They were not nervous; they didn't falter; they didn't search for words, they never showed one ounce of discomfort, and their confidence and surety were literally intoxicating. Now look back and ask yourself, how was this person so good at seducing me? The answer is obvious. This is what their definition of love is, a seduction to derive pleasure, and nothing more. A carefully constructed dance, which allows you to be an instant dance partner, and allows your performance to look like you had been waiting to perform that routine all your life. Magic.

Consider this, if you never had to worry about long-term consequences, never considered moral obligations, no religious judgment, if everything you knew of love was erased so that all your focus were placed on the initial mating process, you could also seduce anyone that showed they were attracted to you. This, like the four-leaf clover, is what happens when certain common DNA or even a small amount of healthy brain functioning is absent.

The very removal allows for the change we were attracted to. The difference is, however, when there is no empathy present, there is only now and right now at that. There is no long-term. When empathy is introduced, we believe that if this is the beginning; the rest is going to be phenomenal. Our empathy was feeling their fervent desire to mate with us, and it was irresistible. Now ask yourself this: why was it irresistible? Why didn't I detect it was all a construct to seduce me? And the answer is, they are pathological.

In simple terms, they believe their own lies, and therefore, they were being genuine and not lying.

BUT... What about us?

Maybe we are lying to ourselves? Let's quickly talk about codependency.

"Codependency is a psychological concept that refers to people who feel extreme amounts of dependence on certain loved ones in their lives, and who feel responsible for the feelings and actions of those loved ones. Codependency is not recognized as a distinct personality disorder by any version of the DSM, including the DSM-5, the most recent version."

That said, research shows that, while codependency does overlap with other personality disorders, it appears to make up a distinct psychological construct. The best way to learn about codependency is to review some signs of codependency." (Credit: Positive Psychology)

The following page contains a list of known symptoms of codependency. That being said, below are some examples of being codependent you might identify with:

- Your value or self-worth is based on whether someone else chooses you or leaves you.

- You would rather suffer occasional abuse from someone, rather than lose them.

- You find it easier than most to understand or cope with someone else's abuse towards you while making excuses for their abusive behavior.

- You find maintaining personal boundaries difficult but observing someone else's boundaries is necessary.

- You apologize for being angry as a reaction to someone's harmful or abusive actions.

- You fear abandonment yet seem to only pick partners that will abandon you.

- You wish they would become the person they were when you first met. You deny the fact that this is the actual person you met, pretending to be someone else.

A simple internet search would yield thousands of these examples, yet all point to the same thing. An inner child wound that fears abandonment. This condition is the most attractive quality for toxic people to mate with.

Without this codependency condition present, you would not tolerate their toxic abusive behaviors. So, if you identify with any of these examples, a good warning sign is feeling butterflies or extreme chemistry with a new mate. The chemistry is with your codependency, not your heart.

What does codependency actually look like?

20 Signs of Codependency

Some things that have been found to correlate with codependency include (Marks et al., 2012):

- Low self-esteem;
- Low levels of narcissism.
- Familial dysfunction.
- Depression.
- Anxiety.
- Stress.

- Low emotional expressivity.

Other signs of codependency include (Lancer, 2016; Mental Health America, n.d.):

- Having a tough time saying no.
- Having poor boundaries.
- Showing emotional reactivity.
- Feeling compelled to take care of people.
- Needing control, especially over others.
- Having trouble communicating honestly.
- Fixating on mistakes.
- Feeling a need to be liked by everyone.
- Feeling a need to always be in a relationship.
- Denying one's own needs, thoughts, and feelings.
- Having intimacy issues.
- Confusing love and pity.
- Displaying fear of abandonment.

A trained professional is needed to help guide you through these issues, and ultimately find the root of the problem and rid you of this or, at a minimum, help you manage your codependency and abandonment issues.

Chapter 3
The Hunt for Love

A pathological liar is someone that absolutely believes in their own lies. If the person you were meeting has no other definition of love other than some maladapted definition, they absolutely believe what they are doing is actual love. If you have empathy, then that feeling is transferred to your own feelings. You experience it as if it were your own. Consider that every brain study of people on heroin and or cocaine exactly matches those that are falling in love. Read on to learn about dopamine, the root of all habits.

Why didn't your empathy detect the dishonesty sooner? Empathy is not a lie detector; it is a sincerity detector. Pathological liars can pass a lie detector test, simply because they are not lying. They believe "their" truth, even if it is outright falsity. Being a narcissistic person changes the very perception of what genuine love is. To them, love is simply pleasure and nothing more. Your empathy detected their pleasure and their anger.

When you absorb brain-altering substances (alcohol, heroin, opiates, cocaine, etc.) they have one purpose: to increase or even maximize the brain's pleasure chemical, dopamine. Dopamine is a chemical that inspires hunting, eating, and mating. Hundreds of thousands of years of evolution made us survivors. We forget there was a time when there was no language, no religion, and no tools of any kind. We were hunter/gatherers that existed like the rest of nature, meaning we ate and procreated. When you are hungry, you seek food, when you are ready to mate, you seek potential mates. Endorphins give us the energy to do these things, and when we achieve each goal, the brain rewards us with a small amount of dopamine as a reward. It is a reward simply because it "feels" good when it happens.

When we do something that feels good, we want to repeat it. When we experience massive dopamine production, we enter "euphoria." Once in a Euphoric State, we no longer have danger deterrents, meaning all the natural red flags or danger signs we would normally consider magically disappear. This is why it is so dangerous to operate a vehicle while under the influence of these substances. It is not the actual substance that is dangerous, it is the dopamine effect it gives us that is the danger. It is not dangerous to transport two cases of wine in your car trunk, it only becomes dangerous when you are transporting it inside your body.

All healthy humans have depended on either testosterone or estrogen. These naturally produced chemicals drive our lust to hunt for food and to mate. They give us endorphins which give us the desire to go out to hunt and also seek a mating partner. Once a suitable partner is found, the hunt has ended, and the process turns into a production of dopamine, a reward. The more suitable the partner is, the more dopamine you receive. The rush of dopamine causes both parties to enter a state of euphoria.

You can compare this state of euphoria to the effects of heroin, cocaine, or alcohol. You are literally high as a kite. That is why your normal defenses lowered. As you know, people that are intoxicated will do some dangerous things without ever considering the consequences. The other unfortunate effect of having such a dopamine rush is the formation of an instant habit. We will define what habits are in the next part. For now, we simply say that any habit repeated too many times that results in massive dopamine is equivalent to an addiction.

When you met your "toxic" ex-partner, they were not being intentionally toxic or habit-forming. Most brain disorders that will cause long-term bonding issues do not have any deficiency in either testosterone or estrogen. Both of you felt the euphoria. It was real for sure, and that is why it felt so real, because it was a normal part of a perfect mating ritual that has been going on for thousands of years. Both of you let down your guard and raised your hopes that you finally met that one person who genuinely wants to be with you forever. Euphoria abounds. So, what happened?

The Karmic Mate

We all have looked for our soul mate. This magical twin flame that sees the world as we do, feels the way we do, and cannot ever leave us. While this is a wonderful fantasy, what I believe we are really hoping for is someone that makes all the pain disappear.

If you are codependent, then perhaps you should look at a soul mate as a temporary mate. Toxic people can smell a codependent person from a mile away. The chemical interaction between a narcissistic person and a codependent person is almost magical at first. I used to believe that narcissistic people were very transactional. Meaning they will do nothing without some sort of selfish reward. I have since corrected that view to believe that narcissistic people are exceptionally good at taking advantage of codependent people, and that codependency makes people very transactional.

Codependency tells us that we are not enough for someone, so we must do something to earn love. If that is your mindset, then you will offer acts of service to earn love, and that is not love. That is a transaction, an emotional barter system. This for that.

In order to fix a broken bone, sometimes it must be re-broken to set it correctly. To become strong, you must tear down muscle so it can rebuild stronger. To cure cancer you might need chemo, which will hurt you to the point you almost die, just to kill the cancer cells, then you can recover without it.

If you are codependent looking for a soul mate, perhaps what you need is a temporary karmic mate. You have survived on coping skills that were not helping you heal from your codependency. In fact, they were enabling your codependency. Allowing you to lower your boundaries and accept that you alone were not enough to be loved, so you offered to sacrifice your boundaries in return for love.

It is only when the right toxic person entered your life and truly betrayed you, caused you so much pain, frustrated you, and almost ended you that you finally took a stand and said, "no more."

You thought this was your soulmate, but perhaps this person was in your life to facilitate the end of your codependency that you could not heal on your own. Like chemo, or the gym, they have shown you that they will not love you no matter what you do for them. They have also shown you proof that you will love them regardless of what they do to you. Perhaps this is the real lesson you needed to finally understand your codependent thoughts are not real, and love is not based on what you do for them or not. They either love you or they do not. Once you learn this lesson, you will be ready for your true soul mate.

Try to think of this horrible person as the door bouncer to your soul mate. They make sure you stay in line and do not jump to a healthy relationship until you are emotionally ready. In other words, just because you want a fantastic mate, does not mean you are entitled to or could actually have one until you are ready. This toxic relationship has caused you to finally seek the resolution to internal conflicts you might have needed to resolve your whole life.

Chapter 4
From Habit to Addiction

Why are you in pain and they do not seem to be in any?

Story time. I went camping in upstate New York with some friends. As nighttime fell upon us, it became very cold. Fortunately, we had chosen a spot that had been used before we got there by other campers. There was a circle of rocks, with a pile of twigs and leaves in the middle of them that was used for a campfire by someone else. We gathered some additional wood, threw it on the leaves, and lit a fire to get warm.

What we did not know, is that there was a harmless snake hiding under the leaves. The weight of the wood, the rocks, and the fire trapped the snake. As the fire grew, the poor snake was getting burned and could not escape.

I decided to reach down and try to save the snake. The snake bit my hand, and so I instinctually withdrew. Then I reached down again to save the snake. It bit me again. As I attempted to help the snake a third time, my friend exclaimed, "Adam, are you stupid? Every time you reach for that damn snake, it will bite you."

I looked at my friends and said these words, "It is the very nature of the snake to strike. The snake is in pain. It is cold-blooded and has no emotions or empathy. The snake cannot tell the difference between the fire, the rocks, or my hand. It only knows it is in pain."

One friend then replied, "So why try to save something that bites you?" My response was simple:
"The fact that the nature of the snake is to strike does not change my nature, which is to help the snake."

At this point, you may think the moral of this story is to stop feeding things that bite you. Perhaps you recognize the snake as your toxic mate, and you trying to save them. The moral of this story is not whether snakes are bad, and people are good. The moral for the purpose of this book is this:

If you are of the habit or it is your nature to help injured cold-blooded animals and or people without empathy, then perhaps you should learn about them, and how to handle them properly so you will not get bitten.

Obviously, non-empathetic creatures like the snake (reptiles, fish, spiders, bugs, narcissistic people) exist everywhere, and that does not change just because we like some and not others. They do not concern themselves with your opinion of their existence, they simply exist. In fact, many people actually enjoy being around them, identify with them and keep them as pets.

Oddly, I believe my nature to help the snake comes from wishing so many times that someone would have helped me. Not because they would get something for it, simply out of kindness.

To answer your next question, I grabbed a long stick and used it safely to extract the snake from danger, and watched it slither away. **End story.**

Habits form by repeating the same thing frequently while receiving emotional rewards each time. The presence of extreme pain or pleasure form instant habits. When a habit is generating or withdrawing dopamine continuously, it becomes an addiction. Instead of looking at drug addiction, let's work it in reverse. If you touch a hot stove, the pain is so intense, along with the emotional negativity, that it causes an instant addiction. It should forever addict you to NOT touching a hot stovetop again for the rest of your life. No need to try that twice. This habit is now permanent because it also sets your belief about it in stone. The pain of touching the stove drained every bit of dopamine from your body in an instant, so your brain has learned to not ever do that again. The belief that it hurts too much is solid and is never needed to re-occur. You would fight as though your life depended on not touching that stovetop.

The reverse effect of this is also true when addicted to things that result in pleasure. If something were to give you a level of pleasure, conversely equal to the amount of pain a stovetop could supply, you would instantly become addicted to doing that over and over again. It would override all your cautionary habits and demand to do it again, regardless of the potentially negative consequences. Therefore, so many people become addicted to heroin after just one try. It supplies the maximum amount of pleasure by exceeding every normal level of dopamine production in an instant. The actual opposite of touching a stovetop is an instant addiction.

Let's discuss something more applicable, hoping you have never even tried heroin. Here is a brief discussion about alcohol. Alcohol is ethanol, also known as ethyl alcohol. After it enters your digestive system, it takes a ride in your bloodstream, passes through cell membranes, and strolls through the heart. It especially likes to hang out in the brain, where it becomes a central nervous system depressant.

While in the brain, ethanol wanders around, **causing feel-good dopamine** to be released and linking up with nerve receptors.

Alcohol is different in that it normally will not create an instant addiction. Alcohol speeds up dopamine addiction at a much slower pace than opiates and heroin. When consuming your first drink, possibly just a shot, regardless of whether you like how it tastes, it releases a small boost of dopamine. As they say, I drink to forget. Forget what you ask? Trauma, stress, problems. Despite the problems, the release of dopamine is pleasurable. The reward of dopamine creates a desire to do it again and repeatedly. The problem is that like heroin, anything that lends stimulus to the brain that produces a dopamine rush quickly adjusts to a new norm.

This results in needing increased amounts of the stimulus just to receive the same reward as the lesser amount provided before. I need to remind you it is not the actual alcohol that is needed, that is merely the stimulus. The desire and need are driven by the craving for an elevated level of dopamine. All these stimuli act essentially the same way. They reteach the brain that maximum amounts of dopamine are now needed to function. Someone wrongfully named these people after the stimuli and not the effect, in my humble opinion, that is. They should all be called dopamine addicts. An unfortunate side effect that these stimuli have in common is that the more quantity they consume, the more they are killing themselves. The body cannot process too much opiate, heroin, or alcohol. They are essentially poison hidden as pleasure.

At this point, you are asking yourself why in the world is this author making me read about all of this addiction stuff when all I need is an answer to stop thinking about this toxic person and heal my heartache?

The answer is something no addict wants to admit, but also the most important part of the healing process. You admit that you are suffering from the dopamine addict this toxic person has turned you into. All addicts will say, I am not addicted, I just have this other problem. I just am coping with a loss, an unpleasant work situation, a lousy marriage, a heartache. Anything but the truth that they still crave the stimuli that gave them dopamine. No one wants to admit they crave poison to fix their depression. So, they isolate, lie about how they are feeling, and become professional victims. Most do not understand how they got addicted in the first place, since many others that have had none of these problems enjoyed the same activity.

Let's remember the organic purpose of dopamine. It is an internal reward, to reinforce good habits and shed bad ones. Not morally good, since our dopamine rewards were created long before morals. These are things that would ensure the survival of the human species. Therefore, if you receive some dopamine when you find a potential mate, imagine how much dopamine you would receive for finding the absolute best perfect mate of a lifetime. It is the equivalent of injecting heroin into your body. Instant addiction.

You didn't do anything wrong; you didn't break any rules, you just went on a date. Now please look back on that date with this perception. We know eating food gives us dopamine, alcohol gives us dopamine and finding a mate gives us dopamine. Dopamine is highly addictive, as discussed. Your date? A restaurant that provided the food, alcohol to lower your boundaries, and the absolute perfect mate to share it with. The perfect dopamine storm, all interpreted as a soul-changing event. Welcome to the beginning of a life-changing addiction that would only grow stronger over an abbreviated time period.

Now consider this logic, partly adapted from a successful program named The Sober Exposure. Years after an alcoholic has stopped drinking alcohol, they still want to drink alcohol. That is why some mistakenly say, once an alcoholic, always an alcoholic. This is not true, as you will learn soon enough that addiction is nothing more than a habit. It is a neural pathway built on the reward and withdrawal of dopamine. All habits are designed this way. When you are an alcoholic, you train your brain a habit to satisfy your normal human thirst for water by drinking alcohol. This is now your habit, a bond with alcohol as a solution to a problem. What are the problems? One, you are thirsty, two you have stress, and three, life in general.

After you form the habit itself, it creates its own problem; you need more alcohol to relieve the problems you started drinking to avoid in the first place, thus addiction. So, years later, if that habit is not switched to a new neural pathway, a new habit, so to speak, then the old one persists. Humans require water, we get thirsty all the time. The alcoholic's brain reaches for the habit of consuming alcohol for a reward when it only requires water. The alcoholic must become like most of us and return to being "addicted" to drinking water. Then the addict will not seek alcohol to satisfy the craving any longer.

A quick note about the brain efficiency. Your brain performs many complex actions simultaneously and without thinking about them. All those bodily functions, all those thoughts, emotions, movement. Examine the best robot in the world, even with all the present technology, scientists cannot make a robot move fluently. Your brain works on electricity and is the most efficient computer on earth. To duplicate what your brain functions perform, would take a computer that draws over five gigawatts of power. The average nuclear power plant only produces two gigawatts of power. Your brain, however, functions with only 20 watts. In order to perform consistently with such minimum power, it needs to be extremely efficient. This is the flaw that allows addiction. If a brain feels rewarded for something, it does not waste energy contemplating whether it is a good thing. The result is a new habit that it relies upon regardless of toxicity.

When you are in a toxic relationship, the relationship was adding and withdrawing the same quantities of dopamine as alcohol does. The constant on-and-off cycle of toxicity created a new habit of reward and withdrawal. The relationship with a toxic person rarely ends peacefully, and normally during a tumultuous time, while we drain dopamine to dangerous levels. The Toxic person then does the unthinkable: they quit the relationship and move on. Leaving you feeling horrible, with no way to recharge your dopamine or feel good.

Somehow, we forget we are even human and need affection. We are so used to using our empathy and sensitivity to measure the relationship that we forget to address our own needs and emotions. So, there you are, heartbroken, betrayed, and left to yourself to solve this dilemma. You start thinking of going back, of fixing it one more time.

This is not actually what you want. You crave attention, intimacy, validation, affection, and compassion.

Unfortunately, you have accidentally created a neural pathway, a habit, or an addiction, to the stimulus of the toxic person. Yes, your brain thinks going back is the answer because that is the habit that was formed so many times, your brain does not know another way. Just like the alcoholic, you must form a new neural pathway (HABIT) to get rid of the old one. This is what you are doing right now by reading this and then completing the program that follows.

Chapter 5
Why Did it fail?

So, with all this dopamine floating around our heads, why did it stop? How could it all turn so bad? The next part of human evolution is where you turned into the perfect mate, and they turned into the four-leaf clover we discussed before.

The body normally rejects anything that gives it too much dopamine, simply because it knows that elevated levels of dopamine are not sustainable over prolonged periods of time. It is a short-term reward. Anything that drains the level of dopamine is painful (the hot stove) and frustrates you. Dopamine is supplied to reward you for obtaining what you desire, not to keep what you desired.

Substantial amounts of dopamine are meant for enormous achievements. Graduating school, getting married, winning the big game, surviving what could have instantly ended you. Because these events happen rarely, they are normally not addictive. Toxic relationships with drugs, alcohol, and even narcissistic people give you a shortcut to the celebratory dopamine with no actual achievement. That is how the addiction starts. A hack, a shortcut to feeling great without merit. Suddenly there is no great need to accomplish anything required to feel great, just drink this, smoke that, or be with this one person and your body feels like you just won the Olympics. Soon enough, you do nothing substantial. You only seek the rewarding feeling, not the challenges of life that reward you.

For example, around the holidays you are so filled with the anticipation of the holiday feast; you brag about how you will eat all day and never stop until they drag you away from the table. The endorphins getting ready for the hunt. We don't have to hunt anymore per se, but we have to wait till it is ready to be eaten. Then, once it is ready, and you smell it, your dopamine kicks in. You now know you will get what you desire, and then you eat a small amount, and somehow the thought of eating all day has disappeared. You become "full" in ten minutes and relax. A new chemical has been released; this one is called serotonin.

Healthy people produce serotonin after they bond with something, and they become content with what they have. Satisfaction would be a better explanation for our purposes. Wait, you didn't bond with the meal? Oh yes, you bonded with it, loved it, and ate it. Now you are satisfied. The serotonin, along with some other satisfaction hormones (not needed for this discussion) are produced and distributed throughout your brain and body.

These new chemicals are also highly addictive separately, they are permanent bonding and permanent satisfaction. That is why you look forward to the holiday every year since childhood. It is a permanent habit perceived as good and reinforced over the years. The very thought of which could give you dopamine in small quantities whenever you think of them. Hence, birthdays, Christmas, valentine's day, Ramadan, boxing day, festivals, carnivals, and Mardi Gras, etc. are all looked forward to as a celebration, a good thing.

All relationships have what they commonly proved to be known as the "stages of love." Some say there are five stages, some say seven, but all say they exist. For our purposes, we will need to focus on the first four stages, since every reference I could find agreed with the first four. Stage one, we have already discussed lust. Lust is driven by the natural existence of estrogen and testosterone. As discussed, regardless of whether there is a narcissistic brain disorder, this lust was not the deficiency in your relationship. Obviously, you both met intending to go on a date, so that part was working perfectly for both of you.

The first few dates and even after, for a brief period, went better than perfect, so that part created the second known stage of relationships called "euphoria." This stage is driven by massive levels of dopamine. Not only was that part working perfectly, but it was also a little too perfect. We will discuss this in a minute. Just hold that thought.

Next, there is something universally known as the third phase as "crisis." Something happens, a distraction, an argument, anything that stops the flow of dopamine. The draining of dopamine from prominent levels is known as "withdrawal." Short-term withdrawal shows up as plain old sadness. It is not a life-altering event, just a small level of disappointment and coping with the withdrawal from whatever was giving you pleasure.

This is the point you need to pay attention and learn what happened to you that caused the trauma bond!

When the crisis stage hits, you must depend on your fight-or-flight response. If you leave the relationship (flight) you will inherently be sad because of its failure, but not be driven into depression. It was not an enforced bond. You merely lost a vision of something you were looking forward to enjoying, a long-lasting, fruitful relationship.

If you decide to "fight" for the relationship, and stay in the relationship, you will then enter the first part of actual real "love." Until this point, what you thought was "falling in love" was just a dopamine lust fest. There was no need for compromise or forgiveness. Everything was perfect. In order to enter a long-time relationship healthily, you will both need to produce "oxytocin." They call it the love hormone, the cuddle hormone. It is not called the "let's have crazy sex and go on an adventure" hormone. It chemically bonds you to another person by attaching itself to a new neural pathway that you believe is good for you, and then relies upon that pathway as truth. This truth calms you down, tells you that you have achieved your goal, and heads you toward the production of serotonin, the point at which your relationship levels out and starts producing actual joy instead of just empty pleasure.

The all you can eat buffet.
Let's look at this analogy. Human lust basically targets two things: food and procreation. You might say no, what about money, power, shelter? I agree, which are all tools to get more food, and procreation. Shelter without food is starvation, power without application is useless.

We lust and hunt for food. In our times, the hunt has been converted to finding a restaurant that suits our tastes. You get ready to go; you talk about it, even obsess about it. Endorphins are driving this motivation. When you are served the food and begin consuming it, you feel pleasure. This is dopamine. You bond with the food by ingesting it. This is Oxytocin. You stop eating when your hunger dissipates, and you sit there with satisfaction. This is serotonin.

What if the person you are dining with says, let's order the same thing right now and eat it all again? What if that person said, "Now, let's go to a steakhouse and order huge steaks?" You would likely be shocked, and reply, "No thank you, I am full. I can't eat anymore. How can you even think of eating more?" If this person consistently did this, at some point you would realize they have an eating disorder. They can never be satisfied.

When you are the proprietor of an "all you can eat buffet," you hope to attract patrons that enjoy the quality and variety of the food your establishment offers. Customers come in and eat quickly and leave. The nemesis of these buffets is the food addict. They do not care about quality or variety, they enjoy quantity. A food addict can sit at a buffet for 10 hours and eat till they burst for a small price. In my humble opinion, food addicts are taking advantage of the business. A regular restaurant would charge thousands to provide the same quantity and they are bypassing the purpose of the buffet. If the restaurant attracts too many food addicts, it will go out of business. Food addicts are "toxic" to that kind of business. The food addict does not care about the restaurant, only the desire for more food. Apparently, just like us, restaurants attract many people. Some will be great customers, some will eat there only once, and others will take advantage of whatever they can.

Now read that again but replace the word "food" for "lust and love," the words "restaurant and buffet" for you, the codependent. It is easy to point out an eating disorder, difficult to point a "love" disorder. Did your toxic partner treat you like a never ending buffet that could never satisfy them? No matter how great the quality and variety of the love you gave them, they always seemed to need more. This is the nature of narcissism.

Let's review the 4 stages of falling in love:

1. Lust (endorphins)
2. Euphoria (Dopamine)
3. Crisis (Fight or Flight)
4. **Long-term bonding (Oxytocin/Serotonin) endorphins and dopamine are no longer needed to seek for a new mate. You are satisfied.**

We produce oxytocin chemically from the interaction of several brain parts.

Here is a fact you might not know: studies have shown all sociopaths (cluster b) are narcissists. All narcissists have thinner than normal walls to their frontal lobes AND underdeveloped cerebral cortexes.

I was listening to a brain doctor speak about attention deficit disorder (ADD), and to make it simple for the audience, he said this, "The front of your brain knows stuff, the back of your brain does stuff." So, it is not a far stretch to say, if both the front and back of your brain are underdeveloped, the stuff you think and do will also differ from the people that do not have unhealthy or variations in their brains compared to the norm.

What I am saying is this: some people simply do not have the physical ability to produce oxytocin, or what we consider healthy brain function, and therefore, without even knowing it themselves, cannot create a meaningful bond that converts to long-term pair bonding. (Monogamy)

Without this bond present, they have an innate ability to detach quickly, move on in an instant, and simply forget they ever cared for you in the first place. Leaving you in a state of confusion, pain, worthlessness, and agony.

Continue to learn about the MASK of the toxic narcissist.

Chapter 6
The Mask

What is the truth about The Mask everyone is talking about?

In this section, we will discuss the mask of the Narcissist. Social media would have you believe that a narcissist always wears a mask from day one. I do not see it that way at all. You might have also heard, "that is when the mask fell" as they turned into a miserable soul. Again, I do not concur. Please read the following and understand a new perspective that might make more sense to you.

As we just covered, there are several stages of love. The lust stage, the euphoric stage, the crisis stage, and then the actual "relationship" stage of the beginning of long-term bonding. The transference of a dopamine lust fest to actual bonding and long-term love.

In the 4th stage, as you overcome obstacles and start producing oxytocin and serotonin, this is where the lie, or something that is hidden most likely happened, as you went into the long-term bonding mode, your partner effectively "lied to you" and said these words **"ME TOO."** This was an unintentional lie, "a mask" to comfort you and get you back to adore them so they could get more dopamine out of you.

At that very point, you ceased being a potential lover and began being "the supply." The awareness community on social media platforms and the entire medical field calls you the supply, because, like all drugs, you "supply dopamine." That is where the word "dope" addict comes from. You were falling in love with a dope addict and didn't even know it. I am sorry to be the one to tell you this if you had not already figured that out. All dope addicts have a supply, and yes, if you are the supply, they are using you as a supply. This is why after the relationship ends, you feel "used" and or drained instead of simply sad.

Perhaps you did not say, "I love you" first? If you were with a seasoned love addict, it went differently. Maybe it was aggressive, and your partner insisted they were in love with you before you even mentioned it. The part that most people, even many mental health professionals, do not realize, is that a certain amount of humans do not possess the ability to convert dopamine pleasure into long-term bonding. If you were to dive deeply into just this subject as a stand-alone project, you would see evidence of several things that do not "seem" on the surface to be connected:

First, we must look at the studies on sociopaths. Sociopaths come in many forms and disorders, but all have a common link: "all sociopaths are narcissists." Then a next quest revealed that sociopaths have a deficiency in "Oxytocin." So, if all sociopaths have no deficiency in estrogen or testosterone, and no deficiency in dopamine, then obviously the primary mating procedure is intact and pretty much normal.

However, it also becomes obvious that anyone suffering from this disorder is lacking the ability to produce oxytocin, which is needed to bond. To check this theory, I ran to look at studies performed on people suffering from a narcissistic personality disorder (NPD), the common link present in all sociopaths, and what did I find? Studies have shown that people with NPD disorder have a unique mutation that gives them a thinner frontal lobe and an underdeveloped cerebral cortex. This led me to examine the production of oxytocin, and that is where I found out that oxytocin production from the hypothalamus is driven in part from the frontal lobe of the brain, interacting with the cerebral cortex. Of course, this is simplified from something that is very complex.

So, to summarize all of this, narcissists cannot produce enough oxytocin to bond to anything. Not their parents, not their siblings, not their children, and especially not you.

Try to look at it as a person with no legs placed in a wheelchair. You ask them to get up and run, and they will point out that they cannot, they have no legs. Then you will say, well, will you run for me? And they will reply, I have no legs, sorry. Well, will you run for YOUR CHILDREN? The answer does not change. That is what the questions are like when I speak publicly to people about their ex that quickly forgot about them and moved on to another, after a day or two.

The most common two questions are, "do they at least love their children, and can they be healed?" The answer is unfortunately no to each of them if they are suffering from NPD. They cannot bond, so their children serve as representations of themselves. The children are to only be used to make them look like excellent parents, which will feed their ego and give them dopamine. Whether they can be fixed, the answer is also sadly no at this point. There is no cure for a thinning frontal lobe or an underdeveloped cerebral cortex.

Will they change? The answer is yes, they will get worse. I have a hunch, however, that if enough awareness were to be made, some universities would produce a substitute or synthetic oxytocin that might have possibly helpful effects. They are, in fact, introducing synthetic oxytocin to new mothers that are having problems bonding with their newborns. I am not suggesting this is due to NPD disorder, only that the prognosis is favorable, and the mothers are bonding. I do not know of the long-term effects.

Let's get back to the relationship and trauma bond. It is only when the secondary process, the long-term bonding that requires the oxytocin fails, your trauma really begins.

When we fall in love, we mistakenly do a couple of things we should not. First, we commit to compromise for the good of the relationship. Second, and most dangerous in a quick-moving relationship, we tend to TRUST, not just a little, but trust entirely in the person we have bonded with. After all, we are in love and have thoughts that this is the one you will love forever. Now we must consider that this person has never bonded with us.

What would a person who didn't earn that trust do with that? You gave your trust, literally the most important thing you have, to a person who did not know how you felt, nor was interested in knowing. This is a painful truth you will have to understand to break from your bond with trauma and find peace.

Since one person is only saying the word love, but with no action of love, the other person ends up doing all the compromises. (Yes, that is you, if you are nodding your head at this, you will have a terrible neck ache before I am through) At first, it is trivial things, because hey, stuff happens and sometimes we need a little help. Each time you compromise, and do something small or forgive something small, the relationship returns to normal, right? WRONG!

They designed each task not to give you peace of mind or conflict resolution, but to give themselves (the toxic partner) dopamine and to simultaneously remove a small amount of your personal boundaries. Like any stimuli of dopamine (drugs, alcohol, etc.) the same amount will not give the required effect for exceptionally long. So, the toxic partner will not be happy for long, and you were also experiencing a small dose of dopamine for accomplishing the task and saving the relationship and or your partner.

This was the start of a habit that will eventually cause you a lot of pain. The relationship then quickly became a series of tasks that always favored the toxic partner, which gave each of you dopamine. The toxic partner received a small dose from manipulating you into serving them and lowering your boundaries. This strokes their ego and, in turn, produces more dopamine. You once again are the hero of the story and saved the relationship, giving you dopamine. You are both getting addicted to the stimulus of each other's actions. What you did not know is that the toxic partner was already an addict before they met you. It is their very survival tool. So why do they suddenly change their behavior and act like they do not love you? Two reasons, one, they do not love you. Yes, that was a little painful to read, but remember, to an addict of any sort, their love is dopamine. That is why it is so hard to live with or love an addict. The addiction hurts everyone around them that cares about them.

They will lie, cheat, prostitute themselves, steal, beg or do anything just to get back to the dopamine they crave so badly. A toxic narcissist is nothing more than an addict. However, rather than a chemical stimulus, they depend on adoration, boosting of pride, and ego being fed to get their needed fix.

Second, why the sudden change in attitude? Just think of any addict that is going through withdrawal. It can be extremely nasty. The worst part is that you are the drug, so by not giving it to them at all times, they believe you are doing it intentionally. They often radically say things, such as, you do not love me! You are cheating on me! You are a liar! They scream these things to deflect what they feel and do. This is called projection. They project everything they feel and do onto you and blame you for their misery. This makes your dopamine drain, and you become quite miserable. After all, misery loves company, so why should the toxic one suffer alone?

You are now both desperate for dopamine, and that is where the cycle will begin again. When any action is repeated with emotion and a dopamine reward or withdrawal, it becomes a habit. The constant draining and reproduction of dopamine in a toxic cyclical relationship form a strong habit. The ongoing process literally creates an addiction, like an alcoholic going back to the bottle. Think of it as if you suddenly could never brush your hair again, even though you have hair, a hairbrush, and a blow dryer. You would, after a few days, crave and obsess over brushing your hair. For most healthy adults, brushing your teeth is a grooming habit we cannot seem to live without. Not because it is healthy, but because we are addicted to doing this after all these years. Maybe I should have just said to drink coffee, but I think you understand where I was going.

It becomes clear that from all of this; the result is going to be disastrous. With one party being a dopamine addict, and the other the supply, there is only so much any person can actually supply, even if they wanted to supply it. Like an alcoholic or a heroin addict, they must keep getting a bigger supply to maintain their needed high. You, however, are in a completely different mindset. You don't need to keep up the dopamine habit; you have something stronger, love. Your serotonin levels, along with other great stuff like epinephrine and cortisol, can keep you satisfied for a long time, a lifetime even if they weren't constantly being drained by the toxic partner in order to produce dopamine for their pleasure.

The presence of serotonin lowers your dopamine and oxytocin levels and therefore requires you to produce more of each, bonding you even stronger each time. Making the "habit" much stronger. The opposite is true of the toxic partner. Each time they met their needed dopamine levels, they will automatically require more dopamine to achieve the same high instead of producing the needed oxytocin to strengthen the bond. It is exhausting. As you get exhausted trying to show a new level of adoration and commitment to the partner, you realize the only way to do this is to lower your self-preservation boundaries and a sense of love for yourself. It is now just a matter of time before you have lost your entire sense of self and any sort of self-protecting boundaries.

NOTE: Ask yourself this: Did they love me, or did they love my attention?

Even if you were to entirely give yourself to them, it would not have been enough. One thing anyone with experience in this field knows is that your participation in this circus is completely incidental. Everyone that has ever loved a toxic person has experienced this. That includes any prior lovers to your toxic partner and any future lovers. So, you might ask this:

"Why can't my ex-partner (or family member, friend) apologize and mean it? Why can they not accept blame for anything? If they had just admitted their wrongdoing and apologized, we would have had peace for a little while. Why am I constantly apologizing for my reaction to their abuse? Why did it always end up as my fault, not theirs?"

A NEW PERSPECTIVE

Everyone has a favorite restaurant; however, we still look for better restaurants or at least different ones. If you agreed with that sentence, you would probably agree that most people feel the same as you. It is only common sense, right?

The most toxic trait of an abusive person comes from an understanding that the abusive behavior is not the problem, it is the symptom of a problem. The problem is that some toxic people cannot produce oxytocin and needed serotonin, so they are always looking for a better mate and are just choosing to stay with you despite your faults. Without bonding, they are stuck in a never-ending early stage of love and never satisfied with anything they have. The lust and search for the dopamine stage is normal, so in their minds, it must be the same for everyone.

If you apply this concept to your failed relationship, you will quickly realize why they were always blaming you for lying and cheating. When you converted to long-term bonding like a healthy person does, your desire to find a better new mate was dismissed. The toxic partner never achieved this stage and stayed in the hunting for a mate stage. Since this is part of their "normal" feelings, they believe you and everyone else must feel the same way. That is why the relationship turns into accusations of infidelity. They assume you acted on a feeling that you do not even possess simply because they have it, and then, of course, accuse you of lying since you are denying what they consider a normal feeling. For this reason, toxic mates are typically extremely insecure and relentlessly jealous. The presence of the core belief that everyone feels they should always search for a better mate creates the symptom. The symptom shows up as abusive behavior.

Buddha said, "I am not what you think I am. You are what you think I am. You believe they are in love because you are. They believe you will lie and cheat because that is what they are.

Go to the next chapter and you will learn the truth about why a toxic person cannot sincerely apologize, nor care to speak the truth.

Chapter 7

Pride Cometh Before the Fall!

Pride. This is the true end of your last relationship. What is the saying? "Pride cometh before the fall." I am not bold enough to say this ended all the relationships of every reader of this short program. However, if there was a narcissistic person involved, I am sure this will be truly relevant.

Narcissistic people live on pride itself. Got a new mate? Pride. Got a job, pride. A child is playing sports. Overcame or got away with a lie? Anything that gives them praise makes them proud and fills their unquenchable need for pride. The reverse is also true. Namely, shame. Shame is something the narcissist will never cope with. Apologize? No. Be exposed? No again. Be blamed for anything? Nope again. Anything that could shame a narcissist is a firm NO. Anything that does not give them pride or feed their ego shames them.

Many people ask themselves, am I the narcissist? Narcissistic people are very petty. They also believe they are always right. Since they treasure pride more than anything, they would rather be right than save a relationship, a friendship or trust. They will sacrifice everything just to prove some petty point of view. You would not be reading this if you were the narcissist.

Now ask why? The same answer as all of this book speaks about will apply. Pride is felt from a derivative of feeling proud. Proud of something they or someone close has achieved. Pride is something that you have personally achieved. So, you may be proud of your child's grades, but you take pride in yourself for raising the child. What happens when we TAKE pride in something? We get a reward like anything else, DOPAMINE!

The addict attempts to get dopamine from everything they touch or come in contact with. Asking a narcissist to lower their pride is like asking a snake to give up its captured prey. Never happened.

The opposite of pride is, of course, shame. Shame is something that has always been the world's biggest currency and motivator. Think about it, as a child… why is your room messy? Did you do that? Is that what you are wearing? Are those your friends? Are these your grades? Is that your boyfriend/girlfriend? Is that your watch? Why are you dressed like that? What school will you attend? Is that your car? All based on shaming you for being less. So, we strive to do better and stay away from shame. Shame is the opposite of Pride, so it drains you of dopamine.

While most people have a much more solid foundation and understand that we love them regardless of most events (empathy tells us this) so, we will lower our pride and apologize for our wrongdoings. Empathy allows us to feel loved regardless of shame. Losing dopamine is not as important as maintaining our bond with family, lovers, friends, or society sometimes. We apologize and move on. That is the power of having empathy and being surrounded by people that love you. You feel bad for hurting someone and hope your apology will mend the issue at hand. If the apology is accepted, you will know because you will feel the love that they feel and know it is going to be ok.

Not the narcissist. The NPD has no empathy, only dopamine. And shame will drain reward chemicals quicker than trying to hold water in a net. That is why they project shame on anything they deem as a threat. To a narcissist, shame is the worst thing they can do to someone and actually gives them pleasure.

This is also why a professional therapist/doctor can never diagnose or even speak about a friend, client, or lover. They must adhere to rigid boundaries and behaviors. They are trained to accept that even if they want engage in personal shameful opinions, they should refrain to remain detached and unopinionated since they are in conflict. If they have any personal part in the subject's actions, then they can not make an unbiased assessment. Unfortunately, less professional people regardless of education tend to throw out these rules and engage in shaming. Isn't it strange how these people cleverly hide behind pride when they do this while claiming some moral high ground? Somehow, instead of elevating themselves, they must lower you.

Why do they do this? Imagine if you were in a battle, enemies everywhere. You have three weapons: a knife, a pistol, and a machine gun. What would you reach for to be the most effective? Of course, you would reach for the machine gun. It is the most dangerous and lethal thing you have, and you're praying that you are better with yours than they are with theirs. When a narcissist needs to win an argument, deflect blame, or just wants to hurt you, they reach for what they consider the most dangerous weapon, the thing that must hurt the most. Shame.

They throw shame at you, to deflect it from themselves, and because in their brains, shame is the worst thing they can do to a person. They apparently don't understand that the worst thing you could do is lie to you about loving you, because they don't understand love, so the worst thing in the world is shame. If you think about all the flying monkeys people talk about, the narcissist will always turn the victim into the villain, that is more of the use of shame, by using minions of people to amplify the shame while claiming to be proud of getting rid of the villain.

Whenever I see someone trying to shame someone instead of helping them, I automatically think of the old saying, people in glass houses should not throw stones. Usually the one throwing the stone, has the most to hide. Mainly their own shame.

Without empathy or actual bonding, LOVE is nothing more than a word that the Narcissistic person uses to get the rush of dopamine. To us, it is a commitment; it is a bond; it is sacrifice, compromise, and so much more. So basically, this addict only needs pride or adoration in the form of attention, and to maintain the important levels of dopamine (which the draining of feels horrible to anyone). They avoid shame at all costs. Yes, they could call you and say, "hey I am really sorry," but there will be no change of behavior attached. Their pride is worth more than anything in the world. For a healthy human, their love is worth more than anything in the world. The narcissist "adores" their pride and protects it with the same force as you would protect your child.

So no, sadly, they will not lower their pride for anything, nor anybody. Not you, not family, not their friends, not their children, nothing. There is one thing I will point out, so it stands alone.

The most important thing a person has is trust. The toxic partner is unwilling to lower their worthless pride, which has an unbelievably damaging effect on trust. They will betray your trust for their addiction. This very betrayal of trust, in my humble opinion, is the cornerstone of your trauma bond.

Chapter 8
Boundaries and Self Love

We are really getting places if you have made it this far. I may not know you, but I am definitely proud of you! In this chapter, you learn boundaries are not selfish; they are a necessity. The program contains some worksheets in step 7 that you can use to identify, set, and keep your boundaries.

A friend of mine was using and abusing me. I allowed it for a long time. I would just brush it off that this is how this person is, but I still maintained the relationship. The longer I allowed, the worse the abuse would get. It wasn't until they severely crossed a foundational boundary that I demanded them to stop. When I finally put my foot down and demanded an apology, they were stunned and acted as though they were the victim of some horrible thing I did by not allowing them to place me in danger. As they carried on about how selfish I had suddenly become, I became calm. There was no choice but to end the relationship. I didn't want to do it; I had to do it. They exclaimed that saying no to them was a betrayal, and I was hurting them.

I looked that person in the eyes and said these words, **"I am not stabbing you in the back. The pain you are feeling is me removing your knife from my chest."** I could see those words deeply hurt that person, but we both knew it was the truth. After that, we never spoke again.

It is time to set some boundaries to protect yourself and your trust. People without boundaries can become quite easy to manipulate. That is why the toxic person was attracted to you in the first place. Toxic and selfish people can detect whether your boundaries are easily removed, and it gives them great power over you to do so.

There are tons of books, manuals, even simple memes on the internet that can teach you how to build your boundaries. I am offering the following as a simple analogy to help you understand them. It will be your job to learn more on your own and strengthen them. You will also have to learn that some boundaries are only meant for certain circumstances, obviously work boundaries will not be appropriate in personal relationship settings and so on.

If your boundaries are too rigid, no one will enjoy being around you, too soft and people will use you. There must be a balance, and equally, you must also learn to observe and respect other people's boundaries, which is most likely something your toxic partner will never learn.

You have the right to determine what you will and will not accept in your life. You can require others to comply with your boundaries if they want to continue being part of your life. It's your time, life, and attention. You can allocate them any way you please. Start by making a list of boundaries that you'd like to apply to your life and the surrounding people. Expect resistance at first but be firm. The important people in your life will comply with time.

To protect your trust and your word, you will need boundaries. Allow me to ask you a question and share an analogy: Ask yourself this question, "Can a Peachtree be selfish?" I know that sounds absurd, but you need to answer it.

There is an old saying that says,

"Self-Love Is the Root from Which All Else Grows."

Let's assume that this old saying is true for a moment. SELF-LOVE IS THE ROOT FROM WHICH ALL ELSE GROWS. It was said so long ago that not even the greatest scholars of our time can name who said it. It was just accepted as the truth. So, if we can accept that a Peachtree is not selfish, maybe we can agree that it also has roots. The roots certainly don't make a tree selfish. The roots supply nourishment from the ground and also anchor it firmly to the ground. Without the roots, any strong wind could blow it over. It could not support the weight of the massive tree above it. Self-love is very much like those roots. Loving yourself is not selfish. It allows you to take care of yourself and nourish yourself, and sturdy yourself in challenging times. It allows you to comfort yourself in troubled times and reward yourself in good times.

The Peachtree also has a bark. Is having the bark selfish? The bark serves a significant role; it protects the wood and sugar veins inside the tree. It makes sure that all the sweetness does not run out, while protecting itself from animals that come by, sharpen their claws, and climb on it. The bark ensures nothing does any severe internal damage, limiting injury to only surface damage.

Without the bark, insects would surely burrow into the tree to get to the sugar that was meant for the Peaches. The bark is actually the boundary for the tree. It protects the important inside of the tree while also allowing it to nourish so that it can produce delicious fruit for everyone.

If the root or the bark is compromised, the sugar and nourishment inside the tree will not get delivered to the branches, and the fruit that the tree supplies will not be sweet. More than likely, the fruit will probably not even stay on the tree. It will fall to the ground and rot. Your boundaries are remarkably similar. They protect your morals, your thoughts, and your beliefs, and they protect your trust, so that your fruit, which we will call kindness and love, stays sweet and useful.

If somebody destroys your boundaries, you live in negativity, and the love and kindness you try to give to others will be toxic. Therefore, the only person who will want that love is another toxic person. Toxic people choose the rotting fruit off the ground, so to speak, and eat that easily found food, rather than working to climb the tree and get to the good fruit. They are the insects and rats of humanity. Do not be a scavengers food supply!

For someone to manipulate you, they will need to pierce your boundaries. Often when we get out of a toxic relationship and into a trauma bond, we become hypervigilant. Hypervigilant means that we see problems wherever we look and in whomever we meet.

Sometimes the problems are real, sometimes they are not. When examining your boundaries, make sure that other people have the right to have their boundaries. This program is not about boundaries, but it needs to be said that it was the lack of your boundaries, or rather the lack of commitment to them, that got you into a trauma bond.

I want to write these words for you, anyone that tries to pierce or lower your boundaries needs to immediately be put in check and kindly left to themselves. I also want to say this: any boundaries that you set serve two purposes. The first purpose is to keep people away from hurting you, and the second is accidental. It confines you within them.

If your boundaries are set too far out, nobody will be comfortable with you, and you will effectively have created an extremely lonely prison cell for yourself. The problem, as I've said earlier in the book, is that if you want to torture someone or punish them, then like in actual prison when you misbehave, they put you in the hole, and the hole is isolation and total punishment. Why are you choosing to do this to yourself?

Another thought about boundaries is that they are not walls. Walls are blockages. Walls do not lower even when it is appropriate. Many people put up walls after a toxic relationship, blocking out the entire world. These imaginary walls are just very rigid boundaries. If you think back about your toxic partner, one of the most disturbing things about them was their own rigid selfish boundaries. Worse, they expected you to be a mind reader, and already know what they wanted and got angry or defensive whenever you didn't comply. I call this the invisible minefield. Everything is going great, then you take one wrong step, and boom. Everything is now ruined.

Here is some advice for you if you built walls or rigid boundaries because of your relationship. Since the walls are imaginary, try to convert them to windows. Windows at least let you see through them, and some can even open on an enjoyable day.

I strongly suggest you learn about boundaries by listening to professionals that know how to identify, set, and keep them realistic or get an enjoyable book about it. There are millions of publications about boundaries. It is not the purpose of this program, so I won't bore you with any more details about that subject.

Please understand that everything in this program is setting some foundational boundaries for you. It will be your responsibility to enhance and balance those so that you can live a healthy life once the trauma bond is completely gone.

Remember, the last thing to grow on any fruit tree is the fruit itself.

Here is a poem I wrote when I was young, before I ever heard about codependency, trust issues or narcissist. I wrote it based solely on feelings. Maybe you will recognize those feelings.

The Web

The spider spun its web around me, as I watched and,
reached to touch the moist and silken strands.
The web was growing large and long before me, and the
silken strands were fast upon my hands.

The silent spider wove its trap around me. I smiled and
watched the way it worked its plan.
My breath would move the webbing very slowly. The spider's
web was not stronger than the breath of man.

The busy spider hurried at its workings.
It never stopped to rest its busy hands.
But as mine reached to break the trap before me, I found
myself ensnared within its strands.

The clinging webbing stuck upon my clothing.
It fell across my eyes and in my hair.
I struggled as the webbing closed around me.
The spider just stood aloof and did not care.

Finally I broke the threads that bound me.
and then I looked upon the spiders broken lair.
Those threads so weak alone, together bound me.
The truth about my life was hanging there.

~ adam.

Chapter 9
Trust

Okay, you made it. This is the final and most important part of the knowledge base before we can start healing your trauma bond. Please pay careful attention to this part. You will need some of these thoughts to complete your journey.

Trust, in my opinion, is the most valuable thing we as members of society possess. It is also the one thing that our parents and teachers utterly failed to teach us about.

Genuine joy can only be experienced by giving joy to another through kindness and love, and in turn, your empathy will feel that joy and make you joyous.

We, as humans, constantly express love for things that cannot possibly love us back. To explain this, think of a newborn baby with healthy parents. The baby was thrust into a new inhospitable world of sound and color; it is bewildered, lost, confused, and scared. There are no higher learning functions at all at this point. The newborn has only needs, needs for warmth, oxygen, food, and comfort. (If you do not have children, replace the word baby with the word "puppy" and it will have the same effect.)

Babies do not love; they only need it. However, the parents take one look at their child and will fall deeply into a loving bond. The gift, in this case, is loving the baby, not being able to be loved back by the baby. The very existence of the baby gives the parents joy, a sense of purpose, and an entirely new outlook on life itself. That is the power of love, not being "loved" but loving someone else. There is no limit on the amount of love you can give, nor is there a calculator that can measure it or add together its value. It might be our one truly divine thing about humans, in this sense.

Kindness also presents a reward of its own. Kindness can be freely given, even to those you do not know, and you will, or at least should, be rewarded with gratitude as a reward. Love and kindness are yours to give, and they always reward most with thoughts of goodness, which produce a chemical reaction of dopamine, cortisone, and many others.

Trust, however, cannot be given, it must be earned. It has a value that can be measured in some ways, certainly financially, sometimes civilly, and priceless emotionally. Without actually understanding this, a majority of people do not value their trust and give their trust freely. Often, they admit they will trust anyone until we give them a reason not to. Strangely enough, someone who freely gives their trust away has shown the receiver a reason to not trust the giver. If you give it to someone that has not earned it, they will betray it.

Think of a person who gives away pamphlets on the street. People walk by and take the pamphlet but as soon as possible throw it in the garbage or the street. That pamphlet could literally contain information that could change that person's life for the better, but because a stranger handed it to them, for free no less, it holds zero value to the receiver. We could lock the same information in a vault and market it correctly. People would then bid untold dollars to learn it. By giving your trust away to someone that has not earned it, you are actually telling them you do not value trust, starting with your own.

So many of my online community feel that they attract only toxic people to them. What they are saying by default is that healthy people avoid them. If you attempt to give your trust to someone who cherishes their own trust, without making them earn it, they will run away from you quickly. Can you see why? If you do not value your trust enough to make a stranger earn it, what will make them think you will value theirs? Why must trust be earned, you might ask?

Let's examine what giving kindness away does. It gives us joy and gratitude. What if there is no gratitude, well maybe we will not be kind to that person again? Perhaps you are very altruistic and prefer to give your kindness with anonymity? No gratitude is needed at all, yet there is still a joy to be had. The joy of knowing your kindness helped another.

Love, as we already explained, can be given to things both living and inanimate. The joy of loving something is usually returned through our empathy, not by being loved back. Expecting it back would be a conditional love, a transaction. To genuinely love something is unconditional, and therefore extremely dangerous, as you have already experienced.

When we love a mate, and we find they do not love us back, we experience heartbreak, not a traumatic bond. Heartbreak is a horrible sadness, possibly one that will send you into actual depression, and in need of medical help in the form of therapy or drugs. (We will cover heartbreak in a different publication, but I strongly suggest you read Heart Math and learn how your heart has its own actual thinking brain.)

Trust is entirely different. You have unlimited love, a poet would say that you "are" love, not just have love. You can give unlimited kindness; the gift is in giving kindness and mercy. It heals us to be kind. Trust, however, is fragile and must be reciprocated to work.

Emotional trust is an unwritten, very formal complex binding contract between two or more people, and a breach or betrayal of trust is deeply felt as a crucial mistake. Remember the words, "it is better to have loved and lost than to never have loved at all?" Well, that does not apply to your trust. Trust, unlike love, is always conditional. If you break one condition, you lose that person's trust.

If you fall out of love, you can fall right back in. But if they betray your trust, it normally can never be repaired by that person. When we "trust" we put our faith in it, we place the confidence of who we are and our value as a person along with it, therefore if someone you genuinely love betrays that trust they are saying your presence, your soul, your love, your faith, all that you are, has no value to them. They are saying you are worthless to them. If you are truly bonded to them and have empathy when they break your trust, you will feel worthless. This is not the truth, but you will feel it, nonetheless.

Now, in a mild friendship, a casual person could betray your trust and you will just stop talking to them, possibly forever. But do you remember the chapter on bonding? When we bond with someone, if we are not trained otherwise, we automatically trust them in full. Remember, these chemicals were not the surviving DNA strain just so that you would have a friend or dinner partner for life, they survived because the bonding was needed to choose whom to mate by chemically bonding to your pack or tribe, to protect and survive from other predators.

KEYNOTE: Trust was essential to survive through things like the ice age and other events. When the relationship is toxic, your bond does not get weaker it is strengthened. Every time you overcome another relationship obstacle; your bond strengthens. Your trust in the relationship also strengthens.

Blind trust is never safe or healthy. Regardless, many people will automatically blindly trust their mates and friends from the start of the relationship without earning it from each other. There are so many other psychological reasons for this, that you could spend your life learning them and still not know a tenth of them. For our limited purposes, we will have to focus on just these isolated items.

Back to trust. When you are/were fully committed to a loving and trusting relationship, you might be unaware if your mate is/was not bonded to you. If you were to think that they were not being genuine during the relationship, that could be considered a breach of their trust, so you avoid thinking that way. A blatant amount of insecurity and accusations from a partner/mate is an obvious sign that they were not bonded to you. How many things were you falsely accused of that could have shown you that your toxic partner did not trust you? Those false accusations alone are the unmistakable evidence they were not bonded to you. (RED FLAG)

Since you trusted this person, your logical side of thinking was making excuses for the rough times in the relationship. The very toxic nature of the relationship demands you must start blaming yourself for not being able to make this person happy. That is what someone you trusted told you, and you believed it. It is true; you are the reason, but not the fault.

As discussed, the addict must have increased stimuli, and you have already given all you have. You have no value to a narcissist. Time for a fresh supply and you become just collateral damage. The silent treatment or ghosting begins. They usually secure a fresh supply before you are discarded, and then the relationship on which you based your entire essence is over. The fact that they can discard you so quickly infuriates most people. How dare they not speak to me? Not communicating is a foundational breach of trust. You valued them enough to hand your trust to them, and they now use it to hurt you? Yes.

I heard this: "They do not leave you for someone better, they leave you for someone that does not know any better." Those words cut me to my core.

They act this way to punish you and get you to plead for forgiveness. What did you do wrong, though? You did not supply the addict with what they need, more dopamine, and they are furious about it!

Some call this the falling of the mask. I see it as it is, a dope addict going through withdrawal. You are now pleading for contact, for love, (more attention) which inflates the toxic partner's ego and gives them more dopamine. Your dopamine becomes completely drained when you do this, and you will feel worthless.

When you miss the Narcissist, and they know you will, you will lower your self-respect to the lowest possible levels and beg to have them back. The lower you get, the higher the dopamine rush they will get.

Eventually, you are the one love bombing them; you are in pain from them; you resent them for what they are doing, and yet beg them to take you back in the name of love. You are now betraying your self-worth and self-respect, and your trust. This is where the real trauma sets in.

You have utterly lost trust in yourself. The voice you have used to speak out loud is the voice you trust the most. People trust their own voice the most since they have heard that voice all their life, through their own ears. Your voice not only speaks to others, but it also speaks to you through your own ears. Since your voice is so familiar to yourself, your brain bypasses a lot of defense mechanisms and accepts what you say as truth, trusts it, and files it away.

In this sense, you are literally what you think and say you are. Since Narcissistic people have no empathy to help them feel other people's feelings, whatever they think they are, goes unchallenged. That is why they have no guilt, no remorse, and no shame. They are emotionally blind to others and so their beliefs, opinions, and feelings become automatic facts.

If you said, "I will never go back to that person" and then went back, you have broken your own word to yourself. This pattern might have repeated so many times that you literally cannot trust yourself with any decisions at all. How many times did you say, this is it! I am NEVER GOING BACK! Your subconscious was listening and believed and trusted you, and then you went back. You went against your own words, and your own trust. Suddenly, you have lost your own sense of identity and trust in yourself, and that is the TRAUMA BOND.

Most people treasure their trust, and their WORD is their BOND. You have mistakenly replaced the value of your word, your promise, and your very sense of self, with this toxic relationship as your only bond, which is now traumatizing you. Hence the term "Trauma Bond." It does not bond you to trauma, your relationship bond is giving you trauma.

I am sorry that I had to give you all this perspective, education, and understanding just to get you to this point. Perhaps I should just make this a video series. It would be more interesting than reading all this summarized biology and psychology stuff.

Please understand this: knowledge gives you power, and your experience has given you wisdom. Combined, they give you the truth, and sometimes the truth will hurt, but as they say, the truth shall set you free.

It is time now to begin the first step of freeing you from your bond with trauma and start restoring your bond to your promised and spoken word!

10 Step Intentional Program Introduction

Whether you read all the knowledge sections of this book or not, this program will work if you want it to. If you are determined to gain back your control, learn to trust yourself, and truly shed your bond with emotional trauma, this will guide you to restore your brain to a healthy way of operating and distance you enough from your toxic relationship, so that you can finally let it go, and move on.

One thing I will disclose, this will not fix sadness. Sadness alone from a broken heart takes time. An example of this could be that it takes at 11 months for a pregnant mare to give birth to a foal, which is the needed gestation period. You cannot change the timeframe by just buying a stallion horse and using him to impregnate 11 mares in one day. It still takes 11 months to make a baby horse. There is no shortcut, however if you are in serious pain perhaps a licensed doctor should be consulted, and medicine to ease your suffering can be prescribed.

Each step of releasing trauma has to be intentional. Like the making of a baby horse, you must incubate a thought process long enough for it to work. Then you must let it mature and grow, and when it is ready, it will turn into your new habit, your new life.

Sadness is the same. There is no actual time limit to heal sadness, but we know that healthier rewarding habits you partake in quicken the end of sadness.

Briefly, a trauma bond, regardless of how complex, is broken into two words. Trauma, something negative happened to you, and bond. You cannot seem to separate from it and move on. In most cases, the trauma was not just a breakup, but a complete betrayal of trust. This trust betrayal is so severe that you literally cannot trust anything, including your own decisions. Because of this one factor, you cannot "bond" with anything else either. Not your daily routines, not a new lover, not a new hobby or method of living, and no joy. The betrayal itself makes people feel they are being punished and should be punished for trusting someone so deeply in the first place that was not worthy of that trust. Now we do not know what to trust at all, including ourselves. Therefore, we must restore your trust piece by piece, and replace the traumatizing relationship bond with your spoken WORD. That's right, your spoken word.

You know the people I am speaking about, the people who, if they say they will do something, they do it. Their word is their bond, not trauma. They identify themselves as trustworthy because they are. They live and die by their promises and commitments, and you literally would have to physically restrain them from keeping a promise. Here is the thing about these gifted, wonderful, trustworthy people: they repel a narcissist like a plague. They will not be around untrustworthy people for any length of time. They magically seem to know when a person is not worthy of their trust and simply exclude them from their life.

An untrustworthy person does not like to be around a person who makes you earn their trust, since it would expose the untrustworthy person soon enough. That is why a toxic partner strategically removes any of your family members or friends that seem to be trustworthy. So, they (your toxic partner) does not get exposed, while having no concern for the negative effect this has on your life. This leaves you with only to the liars and promise breakers to confide in, just to condition you more to their abuse. In a healthy relationship, your partner would treasure and reinforce bonds with trustworthy people and reject the ones that aren't. Do you understand what I am saying? Ask yourself which people got eliminated along the way, and which people stayed. There is your "Ahh Hah" moment.

So how do we do this? How do we become the trustworthy person, so much living by our word that no one would dare lie to us, someone that repels toxic people like bug spray? One word is all you will need. "**INTENTIONAL**"

Before I get into the program, let's talk about the power of one word.

Have you ever heard of Suave shampoo? Almost everyone has. What you might not know is that the company nearly went bankrupt in the 1970s, because of an onslaught of competition and the advertising of one competitor named PRELL shampoo. Prell came out with a fancy advertising program describing it as so concentrated that just one drop of Prell could do the work of an entire bottle of its competitors. This nearly monopolized the industry. A novel named "The Plagiarist" written in the 1980s explains a fictional version of how a single word saved the company, where a marketing executive becomes an industry legend by adding one word to shampoo bottles. They call it fiction; however, it is based on a nonfictional truth.

With company sales declining, a famous wealthy man that owned a large cosmetic company arranged a meeting with the board of Suave, he walked in confidently, and said, "I can save your company today, and if you sign this contract, I will show you how to save your company, double your sales, and it will not cost this company anything to do it. In return, I would like a share of your future profits." Because of the stature of this man, and the desperate condition of the company, they agreed. As the contract was signed, the man reached over to a bottle of Suave shampoo, turned it to display the back of the bottle, pointed to the directions, and said, "add the word, **REPEAT**" right here at the end of the directions. Sales immediately doubled, then quadrupled as they added this word to every product. Just one word literally changed an entire industry.

Words are powerful. Words give notions, allow for thought to be organized, start fights, mend hearts, break hearts and inspire us or can destroy us. When you hear words repeated, you recognize them. They become embedded into our very identity. Repetition is how we learn most things. Two plus two equals four. You knew that as you read it; it is the cornerstone of mathematics taught to you so repeatedly that it became truth.

That is the power of the word, "Repeat."

To heal your trauma bond, you will need to adopt an innovative word into your vocabulary, **Intentional**. You might have, in searching for a solution to end your suffering, heard people say this word, but why? Why is this the word that people say will save me? Because the trauma bond happened accidentally. You accidentally repeated a negative action, and it became a habit, and ultimately a true addiction. Just like all addicts, know that when people say you should stop doing that toxic habit, they should stop. Even though they know they need to stop, a bigger truth consumes them. That they somehow need to keep doing it, regardless. This is Addiction.

So, everyone around you says, "stop thinking about him or her, stop loving them and move on." First, if you were in a mental state that if you could just stop thinking about it, you wouldn't be reading this or asking for their help. Second, you know it is brilliant advice, and the truth. However, a bigger truth keeps conquering that thought and prevails, "But I do love that person, I promised to, and I need them." Where did this inaccurate truth come from? The answer is in the word repeat. Being in a toxic relationship for any length of time made you constantly say and repeat those words in reply to conflicts.

During the toxic times, instead of leaving the relationship immediately, you tried to save the relationship by reenforcing your bond. In hindsight, can you see that this was not a healthy thing to do for yourself? These are phrases you were more than likely forced to speak during the toxic relationship while defending yourself:

"But I Love You, I Would Never Do That, I Apologize for Making You Angry, You Are Right, I Was Wrong, I Trust You, I Am Sorry, I Will Never Leave You, etc."

We not only learn from listening to others speaking words, but we also listen to our own words. Our subconscious listens to everything, but when we hear our own voice, it automatically trusts it and stores it as a truth, a fact.

When those words were said correctly, the toxic partner retreated from battle, accepted your apology for getting angry at their disrespect (which is manipulation), and restored the relationship. That brief harmony felt good. You saved the relationship and stopped the conflict. With a dopamine reward system, this damaging behavior forces our own brain to be temporarily rewarded for staying in an inappropriate relationship and saying these things. This toxic tactic is known as grooming and considerably resembles an alcoholic going back to the bottle. (If you skipped that section of the knowledge base before this part of the book, go back and read that part)

When you repeated this action, it became an accepted habit. A habit repeated multiple times, even because of manipulation, becomes a truth. Arguing against a truth is painful, drains your dopamine, gives you painful frustration, and tries to return to the reward, by repeating the exact action that hurt you in the first place. The action that kept and will continue to hurt you was, "that you are sorry and want to go back to the toxic relationship." Very much like any addict returning to their toxic substance for temporary pleasure.

To fix this accidental repetitive negative habit, you will have to be very INTENTIONAL in replacing it with a new, positive habit. Fortunately, doing so will not make you change or do anything you aren't already doing every day. In the beginning, and the hardest part of this program, you will not have to change any habit, lose any bad habit, learn any new skill set, or pick up any hobbies like going to the gym, saying affirmations, attending therapy, or anything like that. You are just going to introduce one new habit, one that will remind you of adding the word repeat, which saved a multi-billion dollar company and will set you free.

The community formed by "Toxic Abuse Anonymous, LLC" was modeled after many other successful programs which have helped people overcome harmful habits, appropriately called addictions. These programs have helped millions of people overcome addictions and codependency for alcohol, opiates, heroin, stealing, self-harm, lying, and so many others. I was quite surprised that they seem to skip the common trauma bond, but perhaps this program has begun the same way they all started. We shall see. Either way, since it has been successful for all of them to teach in a multiple-step program, the path I have chosen mimics the programs already known to succeed. This program has already helped many people, and I hope it will help you as well.

The following "10 step program" is waiting for you. Just go to the next section and you will learn how to release the trauma bond and start trusting yourself again.

God Speed and good luck!

Before you start. "The Messy Room."

Imagine a six-year-old child having a playdate. The friend gets picked up and now the child is sitting in a messy room. Clothes and toys are everywhere. You enter the room, see the mess, and demand that the child cleans their room immediately!

A half hour later, you go to your child's room to check on their progress. What you find is that the child is still sitting there and has done nothing since you demanded the room be cleaned up. Naturally, you ask why the room has not been cleaned? The child looks upset, even bewildered, and says, "I didn't make this mess. It is not my fault!" You will probably reply, "I don't care who's at fault. It is still your responsibility to clean it." You might even add, "you might not be at fault, but you allowed your friend to make the mess, and it takes two to tango." Still, the room is such a mess that a child does not even know what to do or how to get it done. You might then offer the child some help. The child will eagerly accept.

How do you help, though? Do you do it for them? Probably not. You ask questions. The initial question is, "what should we do first?" When the child says, "I don't know?" you reply, "how about we pick up everything on the floor?" The child agrees and gets to work. Then you might suggest returning toys to a chest. Next will be to put away clothes, dirty items in the hamper clean in the draws or closet. Finally, the last suggestion, "Let's make the bed." The room is now clean.

Did you really help? How did you help? You offered a frustrated child help by **prioritizing**. When we are frustrated with so many thoughts, we have trouble organizing our priorities, so we end up doing nothing.

This is not your fault; you didn't do this. You shouldn't have to suffer; you did nothing wrong. All of this may be the truth. However, just like the child in the room, there is some accountability on your part. In the child's case, and perhaps you also, there is even some accountability on the parent's part as well. The parent left children alone to play. Possibly, this friend makes a mess every time the friend visits your child. Maybe before the other child was allowed to visit, the parent warned that if there is a mess, the child will have to clean it.

Is your head a messy room? Very much like the child in the story, you seek blame and are frustrated. It is commonly known that all mental growth stems from frustration. It begins with potty training, then eating habits, tying your shoelaces, drawing, math, English, friendships, relationships, further education, income, and so on. At each point, there is always someone to blame and frustration. Overcoming these frustrating obstacles in life grows your abilities and resolve. Each time we cope, solve, or overcome the obstacle; we grow.

The program you are about to enter was designed to help you prioritize the cleaning of the mess for yourself. Nobody can do this for you, regardless of fault or blame. It must be you that cleans this up.

To do this, you will need to prioritize. All journeys in life start with a small or large single step. I am sure you have heard this phrase; ***"it is the little things that count."*** Think of an FBI detective trying to solve a crime. The crime itself is obvious, but in order to solve the crime, the detective will examine all the little things. Often solving the entire mystery comes down to a cigarette butt, a chance photo, a smudged fingerprint. Something small sets the case in motion and reveals the truth.

Hollywood also shows us this, a movie may be two hours long, but often in the earliest part of the movie, they reveal a small detail, often overlooked as movie filler or effects, that actually becomes the entire finale, the crucial little detail that explains everything. Please keep this in mind as you take each step of the program.

Whatever you are going through, it most likely did not happen all at once. A casual lie, a passive accusation, some small red flag existed that you ignored right from the start. Some small traumas you've long since forgotten about from your childhood. Those minor details have combined to become the way you think, interact with others, respond and or react to other people and how you resolve conflict.

To overcome a trauma bond, you will need to rebuild your trust and confidence in the same way. It will be the trivial things you do along the way that will combine themselves to form and strengthen your new boundaries and trust in yourself. This cannot be accomplished in one move; this takes many small moves to do. As I stated at the beginning of the book: Welcome to Toxic Abuse Anonymous. You are not alone, and you are not crazy.

The 10 Steps Outline

1. Like all programs, the first part is always going to be admitting there is a problem. This program is no different.

2. The next step is to confirm that you are committed to fixing the problem, regardless of whatever it takes.

   Do you remember when this was how you felt about saving your relationship? That attitude, that you would do anything it took to save the relationship, is what created the problem to begin with. You will need the same level of commitment to replace the trauma addiction with a healthy habit.

3. Review the forming of habits, while actively relearning to trust yourself and bonding to your own word.

4. Commit to taking action repetitively and intentionally to create a new healthy habit.

5. Commit to expanding on your healthy mental and physical habits to reinforce your commitment, and distance yourself even further from the thought of returning to the toxic habit.

6. Intentionally commit to never returning to the unhealthy addiction.

7. Assess your new abilities in a safe environment to validate yourself for accomplishing such a challenging task.

8. Learn to balance your habits in order to create healthy boundaries that protect you from falling back into unhealthy toxicity.

9. Commit to helping others in need by sharing your experience and your wisdom. No, not a cult, but at least instruct your children and loved ones about what you have learned.

10. Finally, go live your life without fear.

Step 1: Admittance

Let's first privately and firmly admit that there is a problem.

The problem is that you allowed yourself to stay in a toxic relationship. Someone with healthy boundaries and self-worth would have left much sooner. When you admit out loud that this is the problem, you will need to say it with sincerity and emotion.

Things we say repeatedly with emotion become the truth, and since we are the person speaking, we trust what we hear coming from our personal voice. After all, why would we lie in private to ourselves?

When you say these words of admittance, you need to think of all the things that have kept you wanting to fix something toxic, stay in something harmful, and now make you ruminate about the past events.

The list of reasons seems to be endless, identify your major reason, but to get you thinking about the perspective, here are some of the self-defeating thoughts codependent, trauma-bonded people tend to feel about themselves:

I am not worthy of love; I need another person to feel complete; I am attracted to toxic relationships. Toxic may be bad, but it makes me feel like I am needed; I am the toxic one; It was all my fault; I am not enough. Etc.

Maybe your problem is solely codependency: people pleasing, speaking up for yourself, maintaining boundaries, saying no, being assertive, saying whatever people want to hear, catering to everyone else's needs but your own, and being used instead of valued.

Perhaps you have self-worth problems? Do you believe you must earn someone's love? Do you do acts of service to deserve love? Do you feel as though, without some action, someone could not possibly love you?

Fill in any words you like. Keep in mind that the right words will make you uncomfortable. Once you isolate the most uncomfortable truth, hold it steady in your mind and think about it.

Then please find a secure place, preferably with a mirror, and say these words out loud:

I (INSERT YOUR NAME) ADMIT THAT I AM CODEPENDENT, I HAVE STAYED IN TOXIC RELATIONSHIPS FAR TOO LONG AND NOW RECOGNIZE THE CONSEQUENCES TO MY LIFE.

As you read each word, hold on to that feeling of discomfort, and allow yourself to experience it without judging it, without explaining it, and without being ashamed of it. Have faith that the end of carrying around these words and feelings has arrived.

Step 2: Commitment

To make this work, you will require your genuine commitment. Funny enough, you will need the commitment because this program is so easy, not because it is hard to do. Like the onset of your trauma bond, you will not see it working at first. For you to form an actual habit, you will have to repeat things intentionally to keep reminding yourself to do them. In the next step, there will be what seems to be the easiest and simplest thing to do. So easy it will challenge your belief that this could work. I want you to remember Albert Einstein's words:

> *"If you cannot explain it in simple terms, then you do not truly understand it."*

Nothing under the sun is new, and nature seeks to break down and simplify things. Centuries of people have felt the way you feel. You believe your events specifically designed your feelings for you and you alone, and that they are so complex.

The truth is everything you are feeling is that it has all been felt before. Billions of people have experienced these feelings over the centuries. They survived and so shall you. Think about your DNA. You are the survivor of thousands of years of horrible and wonderful things. Your very DNA has gone through ice ages and volcanoes, plagues, floods and droughts, wars, and expansion, and survived each time throughout hundreds of thousands of years. If your DNA were not the strongest and did not survive, you wouldn't be here at all. Considering what you and your DNA have already survived, this new challenge will be easy for you. You must face the truth, the truth about the toxic person you were in a relationship with, and, more painfully, the truth about yourself. You can do it.

I offer you this incredibly old saying: if you want to hide something where no one will look, just hide it in plain sight. The obvious is usually the answer, and it is usually simple. Doing something repeatedly, like repairing the relationship that is now haunting you, took total commitment. Your self-sacrifice and determination created this trauma bond accidentally. You will need to 100% commit to replacing the habit and detaching from the bond to free yourself. This will need your dedication, your belief, and your commitment to repeat the process for at least 30 days (about four and a half weeks) or even more.

If you are ready to commit to the easiest path to learning how to break your trauma bond, then read on. If you are not, then stop here until you are. The choice is yours to make, but you must make it, in order for it to work. You must choose to commit, and you literally have to say the words out loud so that your ears hear you say them:

I commit to doing whatever it takes to heal from this trauma bond!

A very smart scientist once said to me, "as humans, we overestimate the challenge in front of us, while underestimating our own abilities." Just because this has caused you a lot of pain, doesn't mean you can't fix it. Just because you haven't fixed it yet, doesn't mean you can't.

Now let's get better! Onward to the next page, where you will find the simple action, you will need to perform and change your bond from a damaging trauma bond to your word, is your bond.

Step 3: Intention

Are you wondering what it means to be "*Intentional*," and why do you need it?

Just to review quickly, your trauma bond is a strong habit resulting from betrayal and a lack of self-trust. The lack of trust is creating doubt where you need confidence. The lack of confidence is creating a desire to isolate, and the isolation creates the desire to stop hurting and return to a happier thought, in this case, a time when you believed you found the love of your life and were going to live happily ever after with them. A horrible cycle.

What most people do not seem to realize is you cannot gain confidence waiting to do something. Simply doing it, gives you the confidence to do it again. The more you do it, the higher your level of confidence becomes. When we say we will do something, and then do it, we get a small amount of dopamine as a reward. This tells us we are doing something good for us and makes us want to do it again. The brain system that does this is called the limbic system, and it does not judge right from wrong, or good from bad. That's why it is so easy to form inappropriate or even horrible habits. Just keep doing and it becomes a normal habit.

So, let's not do things "just to do them for a while."

LET'S DO THINGS INTENTIONALLY!

How can we do this? By narrating our own life, each step of the way. Allowing our ears to hear our own voice and acting exactly as we said we would.

By literally FIRMLY saying OUTLOUD what we intend to do, almost like a crazy person talking to themselves, we will be intentionally living.

Note: Please do not change any habit that you are doing now. Hopefully, there are plenty of great habits you do every day that are healthy and productive. This is why you need your commitment to do this, because you already have habits you can rely upon, and never tried this method with them.

At first, it will be seem so simple, that you might have trouble doing it or believing in it. Most people believe that for something to work, it must be beyond our grasp, and complicated to do. When you fell in love with and trusted a toxic person, it was pretty simple, wasn't it? It was also amazing at the beginning of the relationship. So, you started consciously creating a new habit of loving them.

Now you are going to have to do the same thing, but this time you are going to fall in love with yourself. The expression "time heals all wounds" comes into play here a lot. Yes, time will eventually and accidentally heal your wounds. How does that happen? You ask. Over an extended period, you will eventually and randomly do and repeat everything this program is now instructing you to do intentionally. So, to expedite the time to heal, you are going to do those things intentionally, and reduce the healing time to weeks instead of years.

So here it is:

Whatever it is you do during each day, you must announce out loud before you do it. Change nothing. Try to keep it to things that are healthier and avoid speaking out loud about things you might want to stop doing.

Two Rules you must follow:

- **ONLY CHOOSE THINGS YOU KNOW YOU WILL DO.**

• DO NOT SAY IT OUT LOUD, AND THEN NOT DO IT.

Going to wake up by 8 am? Say it out loud before sleeping. "I will wake up before 8 am tomorrow." Then make sure you do it! Going to have a cup of coffee? Announce, "I am going to drink a cup of coffee" then do it! Going to go to work? Say out loud, "I am going to go to work, and be at my desk/spot by 9 am." Then do it! Planning on wasting an hour on TikTok? Say it, then do it!

Every single thing you do needs this action, the more the better! Eat Ice cream? Watch Netflix, scroll TikTok, read a book? Announce them, then make sure you do it! Literally, with everything you do, you will need to say it out loud so your subconscious hears you say it through your ears (the same way all the negative thoughts got in there) and then when you do it, whatever it is, will force your brain to deliver a small dose of dopamine to reward you. It doesn't matter what you intend to do as long as you intentionally do it. This builds a new neural pathway.

You are essentially rewriting your brain to create a new habit. The new habit formed becomes this: "If I say I will do it, I will do it no matter what." This will take a few weeks to become a legitimately strong habit.

For now, try not to attempt any reverse habits, meaning if you say you will not do something, you announce you will not and then don't. However, if you happen to NEED to not do something, and you know you will NOT do it no matter what, then yes, make it part of your regular program.

Obviously, there are a ton of things you will not realistically do, so your brain rejects them. If you say you will not become an astronaut today, your brain rejects the thought as irrelevant and throws it out as useless information. What you will also need to do is stay away from conflicting actions, so that is why I ask you not to change any habits or challenge yourself at this point. We do not want to test any habits since this is starting a new fragile bonding.

If you are trying to quit smoking or lose weight, now is not the time to test that out. Not that smoking is good for you, but for this exercise to work, you will have to do whatever it is you say you will do. So, if you say, today I will not smoke, and then have a cigarette, you have lied to yourself and become untrustworthy to yourself, get it? No more cheating yourself or things of this nature for the near future. If you say it, do it.

Do it intentionally!

Step 4: Affirm

Let me hear you say it!

I WILL LIVE MY LIFE INTENTIONALLY FOR AS LONG AS IT TAKES TO RESTORE THE TRUST IN MYSELF!

Do this for 30 days (about four and a half weeks) and your life will change. Then we will get to the next step, which is just as simple. No cheating please, live your own life, just do it intentionally.

Need inspiration? Going to quit? Please first remember this saying that you have probably said a million times in your life. "It's the little things that count." Have you ever thought about why that saying is so popular and so true? It is because every important thing you know of and every complex event, machine, thought, or action has to start somewhere.

When detectives are investigating a crime, they research down to the smallest detail. When you watch a movie, they carefully build the plot to foreshadow the big ending, with the tiniest details being cleverly hidden into small, non-notable events.

Every Big River in the world was once a creek. Before that, it was a stream, before that a brook, a branch, which all started with a tiny trickle of water that kept running down the same path.

Neural pathways are the same as every other natural development we see in nature. It starts with a notion, then a thought, then a repeated thought, then an action, then another repeated action until it is a habit. If you repeat that habit enough times, it becomes a routine and then a habit, and finally just your core belief or truth.

This program was designed to help you unlock the potential you already have inside you, restore your determination to do as you say you will do, make your word an unbreakable bond, and enable you to trust yourself again. I ask you to trust the process and see for yourself.

Step 5: Expand

So, has it been thirty days of living intentionally? Did you cheat and just move forward to this step out of curiosity? Guess what, you are an adult, and to cheat, you will need an opponent. However, there is none here. You win this game by being the one person who doesn't cheat.

Even if this were a competition that someone could cheat, I still want and need you to win! So just read on as if it is something to look forward to. It's all good from here on in. Just do it intentionally. Get it? You are in charge of your destiny, and no one else is going to interfere with it.

If you have been doing the intentional method for 30 days, you should be at a place where you will do the things you say. You might have also noticed yourself saying no to things or people about doing things you do not want or intend to do.

Making your "word your bond" and trusting yourself will automatically do this. It becomes your thing. If you know you won't do something, you tell people no, I can't do that. You cease caring about the thing and start caring about your word.

If this is not the case, I urge you to keep doing the prior action until it is just that. I have no way of knowing how deeply your trauma is rooted, so there is no way for me, or even you, to determine how long this will take to accomplish. For me, it took thirty straight days to release my bond, and in those thirty days, I had to start the clock over three separate times. I caught myself lying to myself and not doing things, petty things, that I said I would do.

Any breach of trust is enough to send you back to the trauma bond. This must be intentional and truthful to trust again. So, please, before you try this next step, take a careful assessment of your progress. This is not a race and there is no shame nor judgment in starting over. The only shame would be that you never really try to help yourself. If you are ready, however, whenever that is, it is time to expand your INTENTIONS and start NEW HABITS!

Starting A NEW HABIT

Okay, so most likely you were not the person to do healthy habits consistently before your toxic relationship began. People with all these healthy habits try to avoid toxic habits and live a very regimented life. This kind of life was never really attractive to me personally. However, not being like that left a lot of vacancies in my life to allow someone to come in and fill it up with a bunch of their needs and tasks. I want to say this was entirely random and coincidence, but it seems to be consistent enough that had I been the person who steadily studied, worked out, attended religion, or just had a steady weekend hobby, she would have had to eliminate it to capture all my trust and self-worth the way she had, or rather the way I allowed her to do.

So, what healthy habits can we adopt that will not change our life drastically but will help our "WORD" become our bond? How about some or several of these small commitments to start?

- Commit to going for a walk at regular intervals, even if it is just once a week.
- Repeat positive affirmations every day. I know, I know, but believe me when I say these things work.

Just try it. It takes only moments and gives so much when you do it.
- Learn to meditate and perform nightly brief meditations.
- If you are religious, start practicing prayer.
- Ride a bicycle.
- Finally, commit to going to the gym.
- Commit to reading a self-help book once a month.
- Create a written or electronic schedule of the things you do and will do.
- Listen to more music, learn to enjoy a different genre of music.
- Keep a journal.

It doesn't matter what it is if it helps you cultivate a good feeling and habit. We can find most of the nonphysical things I mentioned right on the internet for free, such as positive affirmations or meditation, learning self-help and boundaries, etc.

Do something you always wanted to do. We always wait for the right time to do something. Most people think they have time because they will live two lives. The first life is now, and it's filled with problems. When we fix these problems and have time to do them, the second life will begin. The thing is, the second life will automatically start, the moment you realize you only have ONE LIFE! This one.

Imagine how much you will reinforce and bond you to your word. If you say you will do something new, and then you do it? It should elate you because the reward is not only exciting, but your brain will say, wow, we are really doing it; we are loving ourselves; we are keeping our word, and we can feel the difference. The old you would never have been able to do this, and finally, the toxic person would never approve of you doing any of this. They would have kept you busy with their needs and wants and ridiculed your needs and wants. You are now celebrating peace and freedom instead of dreading it.

Please take your time before trying the last few steps. The next steps are for truly ending the bond once and for all. They will not be easy and will test everything you have done to this point. Again, there is no shame in needing more or less time. By now, if you have done this right, you should be in a much better place emotionally, and trusting your word.

KEYNOTE: Let's not try to destroy what we have done. I urge you to not try to do any more until you are truly ready.

Take as long as you like, a lifetime if needed. You can literally just use what you have learned as a new life habit and slowly you will heal regardless of ever reading or finishing this program. If you feel strong enough to really challenge yourself, then read on.

Step 6: A Simple Test

Are you ready for a simple test of your word? Well, you are going to have to leave your home for this one. You might laugh at the test, or think it is rude. It was designed to evaluate your codependency and might make you a little uncomfortable. I promise, however, no one will be offended, and you will remain safe.

We are going to test your word. We are going to take a big step, by learning not only if our word is our bond but also evaluate our boundaries. Boundaries are going to be crucial to protect your word. The next step is all about boundaries, but first, let's see if you have any at all by doing a simple exercise.

What is this simple test? You will need to find two things at a local store or department store, maybe a shoe store or a jewelry store. The first thing is something you want, that you can easily afford. Something simple but not too simple, anything you think you would want.

The second thing is something you want, something expensive that you cannot reasonably afford and is just impractical to own right now. Anything from an expensive pair of shoes to a new car. It will not matter what it is, as long as acquiring it requires the help of a salesperson.

For this "window shopping" exercise, you MUST COMMIT that you will NOT buy it when you go to look at it.

Here is the exercise: go to the store, hold it, or try it on, and admire it. Speak kindly of it, and how it feels or makes you feel. Then for no obvious reason, when the salesperson asks if you would like to purchase it, you need to say "no." Okay, laugh at this idea if you must, or be upset that you will essentially waste a salesperson's time, but understand the exercise.

You once came upon a person you thought filled your desires. You once came across a potential mate that answered all your prayers. It wrecked your life when you realized that having them was not as good as wanting them. This exercise will set the clock back to that time you wished for, that time you should have just left without a word and gone on with your life.

That is the purpose, to finally know what it feels like to say the word "NO." No explanation is needed; No is a full sentence. Remember, you are committed to doing this, so now you must. As you walk out of that store, you will know what it feels like to do what you have dreamed about since the breakup. To just say "no" to something you simply desired.

Just like your toxic ex-partner, the salesperson will chuckle at the event and just find someone else to sell the item to without needing any guilt. If you do not understand sales, every "no" received just gets them closer to a yes. Their job, just like the narcissist, is to try to sell their goods to everyone and wait for the right person to buy their goods.

That is exactly what would have happened if you had left that toxic person after the first date. This is an exercise of trusting yourself and building some boundaries. Since you are committed to NOT buying and not giving excuses, you will learn the power of the word NO.

When your "trauma bond" was formed, you lowered your boundaries and slowly turned all your "No" answers into "Yes" answers.

Sadly, you have likely been doing this your whole life. Your parents, DON'T SAY NO TO ME YOUNG MAN/LADY! Your teachers, "don't say no to me young student," your friends, come on, let's just do it! Your first love, "but why not?" "Just say yes!" All your life you were told you know nothing by yourself. You had to ask someone else in charge to let you go to the bathroom. If you want knowledge, go to school, if you want faith, go to some church or temple. You should earn love if you want it. If you want strength, get a trainer, and so on.

Wisdom comes from someone's own experience. What is experience? Well, that usually comes from poor choices. If you truly needed this program, like me, you might already have become a professional at making poor choices.

Most of these poor choices began with you saying no, and some other person convincing you to say "yes." Your gut instinct was to say no, your upbringing and codependency taught you to say yes. However, all those terrible experiences have taught you wisdom. The one piece of wisdom you need to learn through experience this time is it is important to stick to the word and action of NO.

You need to see that the consequences of saying no are not so bad. That guilt does not even apply here. That the ability to commit to your boundaries will not hurt you or anyone else. This is the first actual test of your word and boundaries in the real world. Please do not fail it.

*If you have trouble saying "no" learn to say yes, that you will **NOT** do it!*

Soon enough, you will be with some toxic person at a dinner table, and they will try to gain your trust instead of earning it, and you will require the ability to say no and stick with it. Remember, the right person will stay and take time to earn trust, the wrong people will get frustrated and remove themselves. This lesson is crucial.

An example of how powerful the word NO can be and how to use it correctly.

Everyone loves the power of the word YES. It is praised. In reality, however, often people ask you to do things that will make them feel amazing, regardless of how it makes you feel. Maybe it is time to learn the word NO.

For all these questions, "NO" must be your answer.

Incorrect usage:

Are you happy?

Are you desirable?

Are you respected?

Are you amazing?

Correct usage:

Are you ever going to let someone make you unhappy?

Are you going to let people disrespect you?

Are you ever going to let someone put out your light?

Are you ever going to let someone convince you that you are not amazing?

Do you see how the application of the same word used correctly can change how you feel? Words are powerful when we use them for the correct reasons. And yes, you are amazing!

Step 7: Boundaries & Self-Love

In this step, you will learn that boundaries are not selfish, they are a necessity.

Think about Your Boundaries

Boundaries are the restrictions we rely upon for ourselves in our relationships with others.

Our boundaries can be difficult to define and can change, however, setting boundaries is essential for healthy relationships.

Use this worksheet to define your boundaries. Picturing your boundaries will help simplify where you need to set limits between yourself and other people.

Grab some paper and try to answer some of these questions.

Step One: Reflect

First, take some time to reflect on your current life situation. Jot down answers to the following questions to help define your boundaries.

- What is giving me stress or irritation right now?
- What do I look forward to each day?
- What do I fear each day?
- Who or what gives me strength?

- Who or what drains me?

- Who or what makes me feel good, encouraged, and appreciated?

- Who or what makes me feel insecure, unsupported, and diminished?

Step Two: Inside the box

Draw a box on a blank piece of paper.

Inside the box, list what makes you feel safe and stress-free. Such as:

- Hugs from loved ones
- Walks in nature
- Support from your partner
- Clear communication at work
- Petting your dog or cat
- Having a daily routine
- Bodily autonomy
- Time to pursue hobbies and other interests

Step Three: Outside the box

On the outside of your box, define anything or anyone that makes you feel stressed, uncomfortable, or unsafe. These are people or situations that are pushing your boundaries and need further attention.

Examples could include:

- Your friend asking to borrow money
- Colleagues gossiping at work
- Your roommate using your stuff or eating your food without asking
- Working late instead of going to the gym
- Worrying about what certain people really think of you
- Your partner checking your phone calls and text messages
- Your mother demanding how to raise your children
- Your sister only calling you when they are having a crisis

How to Set Boundaries - State What You Would like.

1. Identify your boundaries

This will help you identify people and situations that make you uncomfortable and where you need to practice boundary setting abilities.

2. Identify your personal values

Boundaries are based on your exclusive personal principles and knowing what is most valuable to you. If you are not clear about your personal priorities, then how can you protect them?

List the life spaces that are most important to you.

3. Practice asserting what you want

Sometimes it's difficult to say what we want and need, especially when dealing with someone in

authority or in a complicated relationship.

Saying what we want is an essential skill for setting healthy boundaries. No further explanation is required when stating your preferences and needs. They can standalone.

Practice using phrases that are ways of saying what you want, assertively and politely.

- "I'd like to ..."
- "I'd prefer to..."
- "I'd rather..."
- "I want to..."
- "..... works for me."
- "I'm more comfortable with... "
- "I've decided that..."
- "I can only do this/meet/ talk on...."
- "This is what's best for me..."

4. Reflect on how this made you feel

When you're not used to stating what you want from certain people or in specific situations, you may feel anxious or guilty about doing so. Uneasiness is normal when we are changing our behavior.

Try embracing any uncomfortable feelings and accepting them just as they are.

Setting Internal Boundaries

We all have the power as adults how we react to situations. It helps to consider and agree to boundaries of what is appropriate or not appropriate.

You can use this worksheet to commit to conduct that you will accept in the future and what you will not.

Consider the following commitments, write the answers on paper along with the "Intentional commitment," and then sign it.

I am going to.... (Choose or create your own)

Be honest and vulnerable with myself.

Find a therapist to help me on my path.

I am going to keep a gratitude journal.

I will NOT.... (Choose or create your own)

Yell, scream, and be demanding of others.

Get drunk with my friends, as it makes me sad the next day.

Realize that these are commitments you will attempt to live by. If you mess up, it's fine! Just re-commit and then try a little harder next time.

Write these words on the bottom of the page and sign it:

I commit to living by the above boundaries I have set for myself above. If I fail,

I will forgive myself and start again.

Your Name

References

- Jackman, R. (2020). Healing your lost inner child: How to stop impulsive reactions, set healthy boundaries and embrace an authentic life. New York: Practical Wisdom Press.

Step 8: The Big Test

If you have gotten to this point, you are now living intentionally and feeling pretty strongly about it. If not, just keep doing what you are doing until you do. This is your program to master and no one else's. It is personal. If it has not helped at all, we want to know, and perhaps you need a different program. No single answer is for everyone, but everyone that cares about you is so proud of your efforts, and you should be as well!

So here it is, no long paragraphs or explanations.

You must intentionally promise yourself not to go back to that relationship or stay in any new toxic relationship. No more thinking about it, no more ruminating. You must end it already; it does not serve you well. You forgive it happened and move on with your life.

Can you see why you were cautioned to not take this step until totally ready because if you fail at this, you will not trust yourself again. Do not say those words until you are ready, or you risk all your challenging work.

You do not need to do this step at all. If you are living intentionally, and learning and practicing new healthy habits, this will happen all by itself. The more you trust your word, the less you are attracted to people that are toxic and untrustworthy. You have become that person you admired, become the person we described at the beginning of the program. Your word is your bond and will no longer tolerate liars and people that do not mean what they say, or practice what they preach. If you spend any time from now on with the toxic person, your instincts will reject them as a friend or mate. You will not tolerate liars and people who break their word any longer. They are not intentional or worse; they are intentionally lying or manipulating you.

For some, forgiveness might have to come into your mind to get through this. This is not spiritual advice, merely practical. It is said that **not** forgiving is the same as drinking poison and hoping someone else will die.

I see it similarly. While forgiving whatever happened, accepting it fully allows me to move on. It also stops me from obsessing that it could have happened differently. It happened; I cannot change that. We cannot go back and change anything, however by forgiving and living our best life, we can change the ending. If you are still concentrating on something, it isn't closed or over, so forgive it already for your own sake so you can move on from it.

As an alternative, if you aren't ready to commit to letting go just yet, let's just try this one:

I COMMIT TO NEVER RETURNING TO OR PERMITTING TOXIC BEHAVIOR FROM MYSELF OR OTHERS.

This promise to yourself is the belief you need to commit to, and if it had been made before you met the toxic person, you would have saved a lot of heartache!

Step 9: Share the Knowledge

When we understand something and have experienced growth from it, we can share the newly found wisdom from it. The right way to end something hidden is to expose it. By explaining and sharing your personal experience, you not only help others, but help yourself.

Because a rising tide raises all ships, including your own, take some time to share your experience with others that might need to know it. Your children, teach them how valuable trust is, your friends and even strangers can and will receive help from your story. Most importantly, by sharing your story, you reinforce your ability to not get involved with toxic people again; you become your word and practice what you preach. If you have done this correctly, you truly have become one of those respectable people that others know will not be compromised, and if you say you will do something, you will. Likewise, if you say no, you will not do it.

Step 10:
GO LIVE YOUR LIFE!

Yep, that's it, go live your life. Go enjoy life in a new light that you never thought possible. Go walk the walk, talk the talk. Practice all you preach. Be the light in the way you want to see the world. Love, just for the sake of loving.

You are the hero in this story and have truly saved a precious life, your own. And remember, be intentional.

Some After Thoughts....

The following are some brief afterthoughts for after you free yourself....

The Walls

If you are like most, after a breakup with a toxic partner. You put up walls around yourself. I briefly covered this at the beginning of the book. Walls have two purposes. The first, they keep things out of our life. The second is a byproduct. They keep us locked inside.

As mentioned in the book, if you misbehave in prison, they will typically punish you with isolation. To some, I believe the isolation is welcome since you are now safe from the other prisoners. However, after a time, it can distort your thoughts. With no interaction, you are left with only your own thoughts, and if you are in a negative space, this can cause long-term damage.

Since your walls are imaginary and controlled by you alone, why not imagine the walls are made of glass? I live in Florida, and the back of my house has enormous windows overlooking a scenic golf course. The windows are hurricane proof, and they can withstand even a category 5 hurricane. When you are ready, you can even install a sliding glass door to peek your head out on nice days. Solid walls for your mind will not help you grow and move on. At least allow yourself to observe the world outside your negativity and be ready when the opportunity presents itself to move on.

What do you want?

First let's review WHY we want? When you want something, it is simply because we do not have it; we lack it. I know that sounds simple, however most do not apply that universally. If you spent so much time wanting them to be your person, it was simply because they were not your person. It is truly that simple. If they were your person, you would still enjoy each other. Have faith in your new self that you are now free to find your person, and that they could never have been the person you needed them to be.

Were you hypnotized?

Hypnotism has been around for a long time. It was always around, even before it was a profession. So, what is it and how does it work?

When we learn something through repetition, it eventually gets locked in our minds as a core belief. As discussed, the brain is very efficient and does not challenge or relearn what we already know as fact. Relearning facts would be a waste of energy. That is why when you hear something that you believe conflicts with a known fact, you become frustrated. Frustration is your brain's way of saying this makes little sense. It is incredibly challenging to get your mind to accept new thoughts that contradict what you believe is a core belief.

Things that challenge your math, your religion, your sense of self must access a safely secured part of our brains and are not easily accessible. Even negative things apply to this, such as I am not worthy of love or success are particularly challenging to change once accepted and filed away in your subconscious as a core belief.

This is where hypnotism can be effective sometimes. Have you ever walked into a room for a purpose and then left the room without accomplishing the purpose? Or opened the fridge, grabbed something other than why you opened it? One last example, you are going somewhere and drive right past your exit or turn? How does this happen?

Moments such as those are called a "perfect hypnotic moment" by hypnotists. During that moment, you are distracted, and your subconscious is actually open to suggestion. No, not like in the movies or some stage act, a small notion. Perhaps something you want but are having trouble with. Subjects like unhealthy habits: overeating, smoking, drinking, etc. are open to suggestion, since the unhealthiness of it is already a conflict waiting to be resolved.

A skilled hypnotist recreates that perfect hypnotic moment by involving you in a cooperative conversation and picks the right moment to distract you. At that moment, he introduces a small suggestive thought that you were already open to in the first place and reinforces it. For example, the hypnotist may suggest you do not need cigarettes and you do not even like them. This thought lingers for several days and slowly changes how you feel about continuing whatever habit you are trying to stop doing.

So how does this apply to you? Toxic relationships offer little peace of mind. Just like you were not with a hypnotist when you drove past your exit, these moments of distraction happen every day. A toxic relationship can be so overwhelming and distracting that if you had a natural "perfect hypnotic event" during a relentless argument, it might have convinced you, you were actually the problem when, in fact, you were not. This is how most advertisement works, convincing you that you want and need things you didn't even know existed. The advertisement is a clever distraction to make you look, and then quietly suggests you need to have the item right now. Then they relentlessly flood you with the advertisement to catch you at that one moment. When you accept the thought, they are trying to convince you of.

Try to examine how you felt about yourself before you met this person, and how you feel about yourself now. Now picture a gold coin. If you find a gold coin, it has value. If you throw it away, it has the same value. The value is intrinsic and does not need your approval or desire to have it. It is easy to understand that the gold in the coin has value. There could be another value to the same coin, such as it is rare. Things that are rare are scarce. People value uniqueness and beauty. I was recently taught this, "There is only one of you, and that is your superpower."

Start telling yourself you are that coin, and you are, and you will always be, priceless.

Reference Section:

Cluster B comprises these 4 personality disorders:

- antisocial
- borderline
- histrionic
- narcissistic

They all have overlapping traits within a spectrum. The 2 that seem to be the most prevalent within the toxic and abusive relationships that we see are NPD & BPD.

- **Narcissistic Personality Disorder (NPD)** - Some of the underlying characteristics are grandiosity or an exaggerated belief in one's self-importance. Narcissists want to be admired and love to be the center of attention. They lack empathy or remorse for how they treat anyone. They exploit those around them but cannot recognize the innate selfishness in their behavior because they lack feelings for others. Most of their pseudo-empathy was learned cognitively through observation and mirroring. A person with NPD doesn't have a sense of self. This is why they mirror and copy people.

- **Borderline Personality Disorder (BPD)** - People with borderline personality disorder are prone to erratic behavior, extremely unpredictable mood swings and highly fraught personal relationships. They have a very unstable self-image, and their personal relationships are usually more intense than other personality disorders, mainly because they have severe abandonment issues and react badly when they feel ignored or un-nurtured by someone they care about.

- **Bipolar Personality Disorder-** This is not a personality disorder and can be curtailed when treated with consistent supervision of medication via therapy and the support of a doctor. This is more of a chemical imbalance. It cannot be cured, but it can be treated and managed, lessening the impact of the episodes. The medication doesn't stop them from experiencing these episodes, this is part of having the disorder. It is a part of their lives and anyone with whom they are involved. There are subcategories within each type, but here we will cover the major points that are important for you to know.

- BP type 1 - episodes of Mania; Must last at least 1 week for this diagnosis but can last for months or years on end.

- Grandiosity: decreased need for sleep, talkative (pressured speech), flight of ideas (racing thoughts), distractibility, irritability, goal-directed behavior, aggressive behavior, and impulsive activities that lead to painful consequences. This can entail marked impairment, hospitalization, and psychosis.

- BP type 2 - Hypomania must last for at least 4 days for this diagnosis.

- Hypomanic following a major depressive episode: This type does not have marked impairment, hospitalization, and psychosis. Major Depression disorder / Uni-depressive disorder doesn't have episodes of mania. They suffer from depression only unless they have a comorbidity.

- One common denominator is self-medicating. This is the way an untreated, unmedicated, and possibly an undiagnosed person deals with and copes with their disorder. When an individual is in denial of their disorder, this can happen as well. This will only add fuel to the fire by adding substance abuse or other possibly harmful addictions into the mix, on top of their disorder. This kind of self-medicating puts everyone at risk, in many ways.

- Abandonment Trauma: Emotional abandonment is a subjective emotional state in which people feel undesired, left behind, insecure, or discarded. People experiencing emotional abandonment may feel at a loss. They may feel like we have cut them off from a crucial source of sustenance or feel withdrawn, either suddenly or through a process of erosion. Emotional abandonment can manifest through loss or separation from a loved one.

- Dismissive Avoidant Attachment: Dismissive-avoidant attachment is a term for when someone tries to avoid emotional connection, attachment, and closeness to other people. People with dismissive avoidant attachment usually doesn't pursue romantic relationships and may actively avoid them. A dismissive attachment style is the opposite of an anxious attachment style. This attachment style often mimics that of someone with NPD.

- Empath: An empath is a person highly attuned to the feelings and emotions of those around them. Not to be confused with being empathetic.

- Codependency: Codependency is a dysfunctional relationship dynamic where one person assumes the role of "the giver," sacrificing their own needs and well-being for the sake of the other, "the taker." The bond in question doesn't have to be romantic; it can occur just as easily between parent and child, friends, and family members.

Made in the USA
Middletown, DE
10 October 2023